SPEAKING

—— WITH THE ——

ENEMY

RICK NORSWORTHY

FORWARD

Sometimes I hated my dad's stammer. I'd be in a rush to get out the door to see my friends, or had to catch a bus or be somewhere soon, and he'd be trying to ask me something. Where I was going, what time I would be home, or worse, how I was doing. Just the usual innocent inquisitive caring questions parents always ask. The sort of thing that rolls off the tongue to my kids without a second thought. I'd hop on the spot in frustration, waiting for him to finish so I could bolt out the door. At times, I'd even butt in and finish his sentence for him, which he hated, but as a young thoughtless kid I knew no better. I can't imagine how he felt, seeing me so obviously impatient and restless.

I never thought too deeply about his stammer when I was young. It was just who he was - that's dad and he stammers. That's the way it is, right? He's ok with it, we love him and he seems happy. Sure, we knew it frustrated him sometimes. We saw that he got aggravated when it took him, sometimes literally, minutes to get one word out. But I had grown up with it and I was used to it. It only ever became an issue when it was an issue to *me*, holding me back from the bus, or a party. If I was bringing friends home I'd mention it to them so they were prepared. Of course, as I got older I grew a deeper understanding of how frustrating it was for him, and what it must have been like for him growing up with it. And with that understanding came a deeper respect and admiration that he had achieved so much in his life despite his impediment.

Dad was once publicly called, by a respected member of his community, "The World's Worst Stammerer". It was a title that haunted him his whole life, and one he wore heavily. Though I doubt it was actually true, I must admit that I have never met or been aware of anyone with a stammer, or stutter, as serious as dad's. It led to many anxious situations for us all when he had to speak publicly, but one of the better moments was watching him give his retirement speech at Reuters. Something he was terrified to do, but had been well prepared for by some recent revelatory speech therapy. Having just been given a state-of-the-art video recorder (the retirement kitty, I might proudly add, being the most they had ever raised for an employee up to that point) he took the microphone and steadied himself to speak. Naturally everyone there knew of dad's stammer, but you could still feel a tension in the air, and could sense that everyone was hoping this wouldn't be one of those awkward moments that shouldn't be mentioned in years to come. Everyone was certainly rooting for dad, but we all knew it could go badly.

He launched into his speech a bit hesitantly, but soon cracked one of his bone-dry jokes and people started to feel the pressure releasing. The laughter must have relaxed dad too as soon he was speaking fairly comfortably. Of course there was still the odd stammer and pause, but the painful gurning, the terrible spluttering and stuttering, the long awful silences that we had all experienced from the man with the "world's worst stammer" were absent. He must have spoken for at least five minutes, with a freedom of expression we hadn't ever heard before. And on his big night too. It was a huge relief for us all and there was even a sense of joy in the air. I think in the car on the way home he must have felt like a million dollars.

This book is less an autobiography and more about dad's journey from the deep south of Georgia, to the summit of news reporting and journalism in the seventies, and how on every step of the way he had to battle prejudice towards his stammer. He started writing it in the early nineties but tragically another affliction – macular degeneration - made him legally blind and he was unable to finish it properly in his later years. He died last year and it was my promise to myself that I would honour his memory by publishing it for him.

Dad started this book in the 1990s and I appreciate that much of the terminology used is not in keeping with the modern culture around stammering, or even with widely used editorial guidelines around the subject. But it *is* what my father went through as he grew up through the 20th Century, and it *is* how he felt. As such, a gentle word of warning – dad grew up in a deeply racist environment, and some of the language used in the book is undoubtedly offensive, but I felt it was important to keep it in to properly convey the sense of time, place and intolerance that my father was experiencing.

This is a modestly extraordinary story which seems very fitting, as my father was a modest, but extraordinary man.

Adam Norsworthy
London, August 2020

INTRODUCTION

I'm writing this book on a Greek island called Symi, which is a popular up-market tourist watering hole in the summer. But in the Winter there's only a handful of foreigners here, besides a few British women who have married Greek men. I'm living about seven hundred feet up a mountainside and the view of the surrounding mountains, the Aegean Sea and Turkey in the distance is breathtaking. But it can get very cold in the winter. And very lonely. And the people who speak enough English, ask me what I am doing here.

"Writing a book." I say.

"What about?"

The first time I was asked this question, my immediate reaction was to say a detective novel or a thriller. But what I had learned over the years about being open about my stammer came back to me and I resisted the urge to avoid the issue. What the hell. Let it all hang out!

"I'm writing a book on stammering," I said. "I've stammered all my life."

I don't know the Greek word for stammer so I had to mime it. Talk about being out in the open! Talk about coming clean! But I didn't realise at the time how clean I had come. I was told later by an Englishman who lives on Symi that since foreigners on the island in the winter are oddities, the whole of the island's 2,700 population want to know who they are and why they are here. There's an amazingly efficient bush telegraph and now I'm known, I'm told, by practically every Greek on the island as the former Reuters correspondent who stammers. My stammer is up front and the islanders speak to me and seem to wait hopefully to hear it.

By becoming more of an oddity than the average winter visitor, and by coming clean about my stammering, I have been accepted by the islanders. And acceptance by strangers of my stammer has made me stammer less. And when I do stammer, it's much more free and easy.

One could not ask for more solitude and beautiful surroundings in which to write a book, but that word 'avoidance' still hounded me. The Greek phrase for 'good morning' is 'kali mera'. But the first time I tried to say it I blocked (another term we use for stammering) on the hard K at the start.

Soon I was avoiding saying good morning altogether. This would not do for a foreigner so warmly welcomed in a small community, so I began to practice what I had been taught in therapy at the City Lit – to 'sneak' up on words. I learned to sneak up on 'kali mera' and let the hard 'K' just brush easily against the roof of my mouth and out it came. It's important to note that this is not a trick, it's a *technique*.

There is an English couple, Wendy and Kit, who have come to stay on Symi for a year and write a couple of books. Getting into my third week here, I had lunch with them once and held several brief conversations with them. Although I had told Kit that I was a stammerer and that I was writing a book on it, I had not mentioned it to Wendy. One day my computer started acting up and I was desperate. I mentioned this to Wendy, who said:

"We have a tape-recorder, why don't you use that to record your book on?" I looked uncomprehendingly at Wendy. She obviously didn't know I stammered.

"The book's on stammering and I'm a stammerer".

"Oh!" she exclaimed, "I hadn't noticed", and she laughed. I managed a laugh too, and even another ouzo. Her three simple words brought home to me better than anything how far I had come on my journey.

The islanders wait to hear my stammer, but when I speak I nearly always disappoint them.

CHAPTER ONE

"You don't stutter when you talk to niggers, do you, Rick?" asked Ted. There was no audible question-mark, so his query was obviously rhetorical. He was from Mississippi and we were the only Southerners at the clinic in New York. Despite the fact that I was from Savannah, Georgia, and thoroughly indoctrinated into its fine old southern traditions, I wasn't prejudiced when it came to stuttering. I stuttered for black as well as white folks. But Ted was a year older than me, sixteen, and he had been in New York for three months, compared with my 24 hours. Was I going to admit to him that I stuttered in front of black people?

"Course not", I replied.

"Me neither," said Ted.

Americans call the affliction "stuttering" and the British call it "stammering". There's no difference. However, for one per cent of the population these two words can mean a lifetime of trouble. Ted and I were among that one per cent. In all my fifteen years I had never known any other stammerers except my mother until I went to the National Hospital for Speech Disorders in New York City in 1947, and I had never discussed it with anyone except my mother and these brief conversations had been only of the "here's what we are going to do about it" variety. It had never occurred to me to delve into the psychological side of it. I simply believed that somehow I had picked it up from my mother.

But.. I definitely sniffed something psychological here. A feeling of superiority could make Ted's speech fluent when he spoke to black people. Why couldn't my superiority make me speak fluently to them? Ted and I shared the same ridiculous southern indoctrination that blacks were inferior human beings, so if Ted could speak fluently with them, why couldn't I? That's what I wanted to know.

What I did know was that I really didn't feel superior to anybody when it came to speaking or practically anything else for that matter. I was sure I was as physically capable of speaking as well as anybody else because at times I was fluent and I could always sing with no problem. But normally the words blocked in my chest and were imprisoned there. To force their escape I would close or screw up my eyes, twist my back and shoulders, clench my fists, tap my foot and go into contortions, making strange, alarming noises in an attempt to make an intelligible sound.

Words frequently would scrape from my chest to the surface one syllable at a time, punctuated by hard, grating "uuuuuuhhhhhhhhs". Sometimes I would break one-syllable words into two or more. I would look anywhere except into the eyes of the person to whom I was speaking. More times than not the listener's response would be a blank or sympathetic look if he were a friend or acquaintance.

Strangers' reactions ranged from uncomprehending surprise or puzzlement to amusement (or if they were children, hilarity) and, occasionally, sympathy. Most times they simply did not understand what I was saying or what was going on. Sometimes if I approached a stranger in the street for directions (an act of bravery on my part) I might be asked if I needed a doctor. If what I had to say was essential, they might ask me to repeat it and I would go through my act again. I knew I was stammering, but I could understand what I was saying. So why couldn't they? My stammer, and its accompanying feelings of anger and frustration, was my master and controlled my life.

It was only when I first heard myself on tape at the clinic in New York in '47 that I realised that much of the time my speech was incomprehensible except for occasional spurts of fluency. Forty-four years later, when I was fifty-nine, at the City Literary Institute in London (known as the City Lit, and whose praises I will sing later) I was to watch and hear myself stammering on video before starting a speech therapy course there. Watching the tape and the expressions of disbelief on the faces of my fellow stammerers, was as tortuous as making the tape and it dawned on me again that I was the World's Worst Stammerer.

It wasn't always a struggle. There were times when I could be positively garrulous. A couple of drinks at a party might produce this effect. A couple more and I might get worse. But it was unpredictable. There were very occasional moments of fluency, mainly among friends. But other times, even with these same friends, I could not make myself understood.

I have always called myself a stammerer or a stutterer, but, in reality, I couldn't even give my speech that high a rating. On my "good" days I stammered. But most of the time the sounds didn't reach my mouth in order for me to stammer. I don't call a silent, heart-tearing struggle for sound or a rasping, grating noise, a stammer.

I think I developed the "nuuuuuuhhhhhhhh" sound for the telephone, an attempt to let the person on the other end know that I was there. Not that it helped. Either my silent block or an alarming, grinding sound too often resulted in a "click" and a dead-line.

But now I think I can call myself a stammerer, but certainly not the world's worst one. I still stumble over words, but I am in control of them and it doesn't worry or depress me as much as it did when I was fifteen or when I was fifty-eight.

Over fifty-three years I became a master at avoiding speaking situations.

One of my dodges was to play deaf and dumb and write out what I was going to say. But at school, the teachers had tried to change my left-handedness to make me write with my right hand, leaving me with an unreadable scrawl. Once I got on a bus and showed the driver a piece of paper with my destination scribbled on it. He couldn't read it so I got off the bus, went back to my office, typed it out and successfully reached my destination on a later bus.

Situations like this would ignite a multitude of emotions that were negative to say the least. The first was fear of stammering and looking like a fool and then feeling like a fool because I went through this charade in the first place. Another would be frustration - missing a bus because I couldn't tell the driver my destination.

The New York City subway system has taken a lot of knocks, but I loved it. You bought as many tokens as you wanted and simply inserted them into a slot and walked through the turnstile and onto the train. One token was good for a journey anywhere in New York. I used to buy twenty at a time, thereby avoiding nineteen speaking situations. New York buses also had a single fare, so there was no talking involved. Not so in London in the 60's.

But I have learned that, for me, the answer is not to resist or fight stammering, but to stammer freely and not fear it. The more freely I stammer, the more my stammer improves and the less I fear it.

Stammering is like pain. My way to handle pain is to try not to fight it, but accept it and to let it flow through my body. Stammering is similar: if it is inevitable, lie back and enjoy it - and it will improve.

Thanks to the City Lit in London, this book has a hopeful and happy ending.

But the experiences I describe in these pages are not all happy ones. In retrospect, some of them are funny, but they weren't funny at the time. And they are not isolated incidents, they are representative of the day in, day out life of a bad stammerer. Stammering is a full-time preoccupation. If a stammerer is not actually stammering, the fear of stammering is there, or just under the surface.

When discussing stammerers in this book, I use the male pronoun because the vast majority of stammerers are men. Celia Levy, the head speech therapist at the City Lit in the nineties, says this has something to do with their physiological make-up.

Stammerers are like snowflakes; we may be similar, but no two of us stammer alike. Some of us speak in a machine-gun-like staccato: "M-M-"My n-n-name is Pa-Pa-Pa-Patrick". They may blink their eyes and slightly screw up their faces. Others stammer only on certain "problem" sounds, like vowels or perhaps a hard "C". And there are others, like me, who suffer long, silent blocks while they screw up their faces, go into contortions and then force or blast out a painful grating sound. There are as many speech patterns as there are stammerers.

Tim Newark, a Londoner, has written a book on famous and great figures throughout history who stammered.

Newark's collection of famous stammerers is impressive: King George VI, King Charles I, Demosthenes, Moses, Emperor Claudius, Kim Philby, Winston Churchill, Somerset Maugham, Lewis Carroll and on and on.

In the book, "Not Good at Talking", Tim describes his own stammer: "I cannot say my name without stammering. Beginning with a tightening of the muscles around my mouth that closes my eyes, purses my lips, and rams tongue against teeth, my head jerks forward impotently. After lengthy, increasingly aggressive nodding, the silent struggle erupts in a rasping rush of air that transforms my Christian name to Dim or Kim or Pim. Anything but Tim. "

Newark and I stammer in a similar way but we do not stammer exactly alike. None of us does. And probably none of us stammer for the same reasons. But like Newark and me, giving our names is a problem with most stammerers.

One of the things that keeps a stammerer from getting bored with life is that he never knows into what kind of predicament his stammer is going to land him. I was invited to a party in New York when I was in my twenties. When I arrived, the mutual friend who had arranged the invitation hadn't turned up. The hostess greeted me and asked my name.

I threw back my shoulders, screwed up my eyes and went through my routine: "UhhhhhhhhhhhhhhhhRick, I told her.

She looked at me quizzically but quickly recovered.

"Hello, Eric. Everybody this is Eric."

"Hello, Eric. I'm John and this is my wife Linda."

Oh shit! How do I get out of this one? When my friend arrived I quickly cornered him and explained that I was Eric, not Rick, for the night. I could see by the amused but sympathetic smile on his face and the shaking of his head that he had just got a brief insight into the life of a stammerer.

CHAPTER TWO

Many Americans look back on their schooldays as halcyon times and my classmates in Savannah were no different; hanging out at the corner drugstore, going to the proms, playing and watching sport, dating and generally having a good time. I occasionally had some good times, too. But not in the classroom.

And the good times outside the classroom were overshadowed by a fear and hatred of school and most of the teachers. I do not look back fondly on my schooldays. School was hell.

The hell started my first day, at the age of six. By that time I was already on my way towards becoming shy and introverted and hesitant to mix with other kids because of the inevitable laughter and mimicry I knew I would have to face. On that first day at school when each of us had to give our names to the teacher my spluttering sounds and contortions caused great glee among my classmates, one in particular. His name was Rudolph and I remember his face and high-pitched laughter even now fifty-three years later.

He carried on his mocking in the playground at recess and nobody was more surprised than me when I hit him in the stomach. He wasn't prepared for it, either, because many stammerers, including me at that time, come across as timid souls. Rudolph doubled up and went down. End of fight. End of Rudolph's laughter. It wasn't bravery that caused me to punch him, but anger, an emotion that was to play a large part in my life.

But I came up against tougher bullies than Rudolph during my schooldays and not all of them went down with one punch - many times

I was the one who couldn't get off the ground when it was over. I'm not a natural fighter, but I got lots of practice. And while practice didn't make perfect, and I lost a lot of fights, I wasn't a pushover by the time I reached the age of twelve.

Later I understood that the anger I felt towards bullies such as Rudolph was not solely directed towards them but at myself. The anger followed frustration from being unable to speak. I carry that anger with me to this day. Not that I go around punching people in the stomach. I keep it bottled up inside until finally I explode over something unrelated to my speech. I used to kick in a door or cuss my dog. Now I just cuss. But I am slowly getting it under control.

I began to gather emotional scars that would last the rest of my life when each of us had to stand and give the teacher our name. The torture continued as I was forced to recite multiplication tables, read aloud and undergo oral examinations. Didn't the teachers realise what torture and embarrassment they were putting me through? Didn't they care?

As I watched my own two children growing up, I looked back and wondered about the lasting effects of a life of stammering. How could I have survived childhood and my teens? At times my children seemed so innocent and vulnerable. I must have been like that before I became wary, cynical and cunning at too early an age.

Whenever I started a new school, my mother, who knew what I was in for, would become worried and depressed days before. I shared her apprehension and fears and the household would become a gloomy one.

What kind of person would I be had I not stammered? What emotional scars did I carry? Oh I knew that I bore scars, all right, but I didn't dare look at them or discuss them until I was made to, many many years later.

CHAPTER THREE

It was the year 1947 and to me New York City was the most exciting place in the world. But here I was, fifteen years old and full of hope that the therapists at the NYC hospital would clear up this affliction that ruled my life as easily as a doctor would clear up a case of influenza. And as soon as I was cured I would return home and set Savannah's academic and social life on fire with my fluent speech. The stammer was my wicked master and it cracked the whip over my miserable life. My little world revolved around my stammer.

Most of the other stammerers at the clinic were war veterans in their twenties and the government was paying their way under the G.I. Bill of Rights. The New York Hospital for Speech Disorders wasn't really like a hospital. We went there five days a week and attended group therapy and relaxation classes. Very little time was actually spent teaching any techniques that would help us to be more fluent. The theory was that we knew how to speak and some psychological demon was stopping us. Learn to relax and cope with the demon and we would stop stammering. Fair enough, I thought. But were they going to tell me what the demon was or how it got there?

The only technique they taught us was to drop our jaws so the words would come out easily. But this was a blanket technique, which the therapists applied to all stammerers. What about me? My words wouldn't even travel as high as my jaw. They became lodged in my chest and refused to budge until I exerted all my physical and emotional strength to shove them to the surface where they emerged, as often as not as incomprehensible sounds.

For an hour each day we would lie on deck chairs while classical music was played and we would tense up one muscle at a time and then relax it. We were told to think of placid places, quiet and calm scenes and learn to relax. I thought of Georgia -St Simon's Island and Savannah and their long, white sandy beaches and palmetto trees. There were some pointers on how to breathe. "Watch a baby breathe," we were told. "He breathes from the stomach, not the chest." Breathe? I knew how to breathe. If I didn't know how to breathe I'd be dead. What I didn't know how to do was to dislodge sounds from my chest and get them audibly past my lips. During the rest of the day the group usually discussed general topics, like yesterday's baseball game between the New York Giants and the Brooklyn Dodgers. Only occasionally was stammering discussed. When someone would ask why we weren't spending more time discussing our speech and what to do about it, the therapists would tell us that we were too preoccupied with it and we should think and talk about other things. Other things? I would be happy to think and talk about other things, like baseball games, but only when they "cured" my stammer. So let's get on with it.

Occasionally, though, we *would* discuss stammering. One man in the group told us about losing his job at a department store. He stammered to a valuable customer who complained to the manager. My friend got two weeks' pay and sympathetically but firmly shown the exit. That was in the days of burlesque and this fellow decided to drop into a theatre and have a few laughs to cheer him up. The stand-up comic was mimicking stammerers and the audience was roaring its appreciation, so he went next door to a bar instead. The barman, taking his stammering for a sign of drunkenness, showed him the exit.

The clinic didn't prepare us or help us to deal with situations like that, or the anger, depression, and feeling of rejection they caused. They would sometimes listen to our problems, but they rarely had answers for us. "Relax and drop your jaw", they kept repeating. On one occasion a therapist leading a group joined my list of enemies. I mentioned that I stammered less when I talked to girls than when I talked to boys. Not that I didn't stammer to both, girls were just slightly easier to talk to than boys. Why? Smoking wasn't allowed in the room, so this psychologist would sit there sucking and chewing his unlit pipe. He was the first psychologist I had any contact with and since then I have I always pictured them sucking pipes.

"Do you feel more comfortable in the company of women than you do with men?" he asked me though his pipe.

"Maybe," I said. "I don't know. Sometimes."

"Perhaps," said the therapist, "your father was distant and you related to your mother because she stuttered. Do you think you have any homosexual tendencies?"

What was this pipe-sucker saying? I was fifteen years old and the thought of homosexuality had no appeal whatsoever and it hasn't since. I gave him a straight answer:

"No." I looked at the other members of the all-male group, wondering what they thought about me now.

"Well you probably came very close to being a homosexual," said this pompous, pipe-sucking bastard of a psychologist.

Now I love women and I like to be around them and I CAN talk to them easier that I can men. I think women are a great sex. But to lay this nickel-and-dime psychology on me in public at fifteen! I wasn't worried that I was a homosexual because I knew better. But I was worried what the other thirty or so guys in the group, including Ted, with whom I shared a room, would think. The psychologist came up to me after the session and told me not to worry. But the damage was done. Ted tried to make a joke out of it but I wasn't too sure how he really felt.

Another fault of the New York Hospital for Speech Disorders was that the groups were too large, sometimes more than forty people. Years later in London at the City Lit I learned that nine or ten people is ideal. In smaller groups we got to know each other and to realise that no two stammerers are alike in speech or personality. I asked City Lit therapist

Celia Levy to give me a stereotype of a stammerer's personality. She said she couldn't.

The therapy groups at the speech hospital in New York were too big for us to know or help each other. Or for the therapists to get to know us and the different ways in which we stammered and how we reacted to it. Once we were even told that there was such a thing as a "stuttering personality" and that it was not a very nice personality. They told us was that we were all selfish. We were bums and we had to learn to be better people. I don't remember them telling us how to go about improving our speech. Most of the therapists there were stammerers themselves and they could get away with telling us that we were bums. They stammered only occasionally, but we had no way of knowing how badly they had stammered before. Some stammerers perform worse than others and on a scale of one to ten I reckon I scored about twenty-five.

For five days a week we relaxed, breathed like babies and dropped our jaws. And it worked! It worked until we stepped out of the front door of the hospital to go back to our boarding house on East 17th Street. We were in the real world and we all stammered again.

My parents in Savannah had scraped together $500 plus rail fare and two dollars a week spending money for my three-month stay in New York. For another seventeen dollars a week I got three greasy meals a day and a bed in a room with Ted. I earned an extra three dollars a week by carrying groceries for the landlady on Saturday mornings.

Ted and I were accepted by the war veterans in the boarding house and we learned more about life from them than anything we learned at the speech clinic. Not about speech, mind you. They taught us how to raise hell.

CHAPTER FOUR

The war veterans taught Ted and me lots of new swear words, some of them in German, French and even Japanese. They knew all about sex and would do practically everything but draw pictures to describe their sexual encounters in England, France, Italy, Germany and Japan. They showed us where to find whores. Even though my five dollars a week pocket money didn't stretch to prostitutes, I figured that this knowledge would at least make me more sophisticated and worldly-wise when I got home to Savannah. I doubt if my parents would consider this sort of knowledge to be worth their five hundred hard earned bucks.

And they taught us to drink beer. They said that life looked rosier through the bottom of a glass and I learned to agree. My friend Tom Zimmerman said he would rather look into a beer glass than into a bombsight. At my age they both sounded pretty cool. The catch was that it launched me on a long career of drinking too much. Ask my wife Mary. I can blame it on my stammer or, better still, Alexander Graham Bell. I can also blame it on my Old Man, who was pretty good at soaking it up too, but I prefer to blame it on my stammer. I found that after each rejection or humiliation, a few drinks would ease the pain. I also knew that a couple of drinks before going to a social occasion would relieve some of the tension and help me speak more easily.

I explored every street in Manhattan, mostly on foot. The subway cost five cents and I was saving my money for Saturday nights when Ted and I would go out on the town with the big boys. Most nights Ted and I would take in an ancient movie at a Third Avenue flea pit. The big boys went out every night. Sometimes we would go to Greenwich Village for some smooth jazz, and other times to Harlem for more raucous jazz or to Midtown in the East Fifties where you could listen all night to famous swing bands for the price of a beer. There was a bar in Brooklyn we patronised because the owner was a stammerer and we got free cold ones. He had only two conversation pieces displayed behind the bar: a framed dollar bill which he said was the first dollar he made when he was behind the bar and the other was a shrunken human head he picked up in New Guinea during the war, which he said was the first person to mock his stammer when he was behind the bar.

In those days beer was five cents a glass and in New York neighbourhood bars, every fourth round was on the house. For us in this Brooklyn joint, however, the owner would thump the bar every third round, indicating the drinks were on him. Years later when I came to England I was shocked to see people buying the barmen and barmaids drinks. In New York it was the other way around. Some Saturday nights my war veteran friends would cross the Hudson River to Jersey City to a burlesque theatre where they had strippers, who were banned in New York. Since Ted and I were under eighteen, it was as illegal for us to see this wickedness as it was to go into a bar, but we crowded in along with our older friends and at the age of fifteen, I gazed with awe for the first time at a naked woman. She looked just like my war veteran friends said she would!

On my return to New York a few years later, my cousin Peggy and her husband Tom were to teach me that there was more to New York than bars, whores and strippers. It also had things like theatres and museums. But while the memory of my first visit to the New York Museum of Modern Art has dimmed, I vividly remember that naked stripper.

CHAPTER FIVE

After three months of strippers, jazz and the occasional bit of speech therapy, I went to Pennsylvania station and gloomily boarded the West Coast Champion for Savannah. I didn't look forward to my parents discovering they had wasted several hundred dollars by sending me to one of the most respected speech clinics in the United States to no avail.

There they were at Union station in Savannah at 5am. Some neighbours had driven them to the station because we had no car.

"You've improved", said the neighbour's son and my good friend, Bill Ross, before I could open my mouth. But during the twenty minute drive home it became clear to them all that I had not improved. My mother wept.

The New York Clinic had urged me to carry on with speech therapy in Savannah and my father and I found a therapist who said yes, she knew all about stammerers and could cure me. Stammerers beware: when therapists say they can 'cure' you, it's time to head for the hills clutching your wallet. But stammerers, like some cancer patients, can be pretty gullible and my Old Man reached into his pocket again. Her 'therapy' consisted of making me repeat tongue-twister after tongue-twister. She was teaching me to pronounce words. But I already knew how to pronounce them! I didn't need someone to teach me the mechanisms of speech because I already knew how to talk. I needed someone to teach me how to free the words. I would leave her office a sweating, shaking, angry wreck every afternoon. If I had gained anything at the hospital in New York, she quickly destroyed it.

Winston Churchill had a speech impediment, but in his book on famous stammerers, Tim Newark quotes Churchill's son Randolph as saying " ... It is hard to define exactly what it was: some thought it was a stammer: others a lisp." He had a hard time with the letter "S". Newark says that Churchill used to recite such phrases as: "The Spanish ships I cannot see for they are not in sight."

Phrases like that may or may not help a lisp but they would certainly not help a stammer. The therapist who inflicted tongue-twisters on me was supposed to be helping me but she became an enemy.

In his book, Newark describes his first experience with therapy: "By the age of nine or ten, my stammer had become sufficiently pronounced to be a problem. "It developed into an unpredictable impediment composed of both blocking and repetition which severely hindered my conversation. My first encounter with speech therapy swiftly followed. Overall it was an enjoyable experience, for while my contemporaries battled with elementary maths at school, I was allowed the mornings off to ramble on about the finer aspects of fossils and dinosaurs -- my all-consuming interest at the time - - to an attentive white-clothed woman. However, the keenness of the speech therapist began to falter when she determined that I was not the victim of a brutal father, nor did I wet my bed. Indeed as soon as she discovered there was nothing very orthodox wrong with me, there seemed little point in continuing the sessions."

What? He visited this therapist during school hours!? Of course, I would have taken advantage of this and lied to her. "Yes, Miss Whitecoat," I would have said, "My parents beat the hell out of me every day before breakfast and every night before I go to bed. When I wake up in the morning I'm swimming in my own urine". I'd have gone *that* far to get some time off from school.

In speech therapy parlance this attitude is called "avoidance" - dodging and substituting words and manufacturing excuses to get out of speaking. It is a craft that stammerers cultivate and I became a master at it, whether it was substituting one word for another, not telephoning someone when I should, getting someone else to phone when I should make the call, even feigning illness. I would go to the extent of buying a ticket for a more expensive station on the London underground or, as I wrote earlier, buses because I started to stammer on the name of the station or stop I wanted. Stammering can be an expensive business.

Charles Van Riper, an eminent American speech therapist and a stammerer, said most adult stammerers "made avoidance almost a career." No two stammerers are exactly alike, but we do have similar tactics, and avoidance is certainly one of them.

The City Lit goes further; "Every time stuttering is successfully avoided, the future stuttering is strengthened. To preserve the image of fluency, words are changed, situations are avoided, often at great personal cost to the individual.

"The person who avoids is fully convinced that by avoiding he remains fluent. But has he tested reality? Does he really know what would happen if he didn't avoid?"

But this "therapy" that Newark received was during the 1960s, some twenty years after my first encounter with speech therapists. The City Lit was talking another couple of decades later still. Why had there been no progress?

I am told by speech therapists that one per cent of the world's population is supposed to stammer. So in the Savannah area with a population of about 100,000 there should be about 1,000. Why did I never meet one outside my family? One reason may be that we do not advertise our affliction. We keep quiet about it. But this could not have been possible in Savannah High School, where the teachers had no mercy on this stammerer or any hesitation about making me do my thing in class, no matter how embarrassing. The whole faculty and student body knew I stammered. But I didn't know of anybody else who did. In later years, my brother Lacy claimed to be a stammerer, though I never heard him. When I asked him why he never stammered, he said that he rarely did but was always afraid he would. He spent lots of money on people who were going to teach him not to be afraid of stammering. As far as I know he never stopped being afraid.

One of the men on my speech course in New York was a big, handsome guy, who was advertising manager of Van Heusen shirts. He had a very slight stammer. And I mean slight. Maybe he would hiccup on one word in a thousand. But he feared it as much as I feared my horrible, blocking, wracking, rasping, explosive, impediment. There he was, thirty-five and good-looking with one of the best advertising jobs in New York and he lived in fear of hesitating on one in a thousand words. He wouldn't ask a girl for a date, although the pretty young receptionist at the clinic would go out of her way to tell him what time she got off work. I asked him if there were certain situations in which he did stammer badly. Conferences, shopping, the telephone?

"No. I never know when it will happen. But I know I'm a stutterer and it gets me down." We all envied him.

I rarely run into stammerers and I've probably met thousands of people in more than forty countries and, not including ones on therapy courses, I can count the stammerers I've met on one hand. I was in Northern Ireland for two years and never met one. I was in Southeast Asia for four years and never met one. During my entire twenty-eight year career with Reuters, the international news agency, I met only one colleague who stammered. But then, for many stammerers, journalism is not the ideal occupation.

CHAPTER SIX

Now a stammerer has plenty of enemies. His enemies are ninety-nine per cent of fluent speakers. Not that these are evil people and have it in for stammerers. It's just that some of them are busy people like policemen, barmen, switchboard operators and bus drivers. Others are uncomprehending and are too embarrassed to watch and listen to a stammerer go through his contortions. They simply can't deal with us. Others are anxious to get a word in and don't have the patience for the stammerer to struggle with his speech. Even your parents are your enemies because they worry about you and wonder how you are going to cope in life. They send you on a guilt trip.

Yessir, I had lots of enemies out there in that big, smug world where fluent speech is taken for granted. But the man who was my greatest enemy is dead. Now you may ask: "Well isn't that a good thing?" My answer is "no" because the evil he did lived on. My greatest enemy, and the enemy of the vast majority of stammerers, was Alexander Graham Bell, who died and left us the telephone.

Alexander Graham Bell and his goddam telephone.

The phone was for me a colossal problem that accompanied me to high school and into my teens, to work, on holidays, at home, my social life. Everywhere.

His invention has made the lives of hundreds of thousands of stammerers hell. Try putting your last coin into a telephone on a dark, cold, rainy night to call a taxi and *knowing* that the odds are that the dispatcher is going to hang up on you and you face a long, cold, wet and possibly dangerous walk home. Try that you smug, fluent speaker -

my enemy. Try phoning for a job interview and having the switchboard operator keep hanging up on you until all your nickels are gone. See? You can't even comprehend it.

Answering the telephone, for me, was not *quite* as bad as making a call. There wasn't as much pressure. When the phone rings, the ball is in the caller's court. They want something from you. But if what they wanted was my name, the caller had smashed the ball back into my court and the advantage was his. In all the jobs I've had, the simple company rule was that you answered the phone with your name. I just couldn't do it. I frequently could manage "hello", but so many times their next response was "who's speaking?" and the call would go downhill from there.

CHAPTER SEVEN

But I was back in Savannah, Georgia, and entering a new school, with all the trauma that such a momentous moment in a young person's life involved. Savannah High School had a good basketball team, a middling football team and one of the lousiest academic records in the United States. With a few notable exceptions, the teachers were ignoramuses who couldn't keep up with many of the students. The taxpayers of Georgia were divided mainly into two groups, those who weren't going to pay money for "book learnin'" and those who sent their kids to fancy private schools. Neither group was inclined to vote for politicians who wanted to improve the Georgia state school system, much less help the one per cent of the population who stammered. When I left high school and took the lowest job going at an oil refinery, I was making as much money as an experienced school teacher at Savannah High School.

I can only hope that things have improved. But a few years ago I met a fellow passenger on an airplane who had been transferred from somewhere out west to Savannah. He and his wife checked out the schools and found that Harvard University had graded all the fifty state school systems and that Georgia came fiftieth and that Savannah had the worst schools in Georgia. The state of Georgia said you had to stay in school until you were sixteen. At the age of fifteen I was determined that I had only a year to go. But my parents prevailed and I suffered through until I graduated at the bottom of my class at the age of nineteen, two years older than the average kid.

But I was always polite to my elders as every southern boy is taught. In fact I was polite and helpful to everybody. I always tried my best to be "Mister Nice Guy" and put a happy and brave face on my general feelings of anger, hostility and despondency. Nice as I was, very few of the teachers took pity. There was one incident in Latin class where we were supposed to conjugate the verb "amo". Each member of the class was supposed to stand up and say:

"Amo - I love.

"Amas - you love

"Amat - he/she loves

"Amamus - we love

"Amatis – you love

"Amant -they love"

When it came my turn, something came over me and I felt a fluent feeling coming on. I rose quickly and out it poured-rapid fire:

"Amo-amas-amat-amamus-amatis-amant."

Although I had totally disregarded the format ordered by the teacher and followed by my fluent classmates, I had got the essential words out and showed her I knew my stuff. I sat down quietly satisfied that I had shown my classmates I *could* speak without stammering. Albeit very very rarely.

"Now Richard," she said sternly, "what makes you think you can get away with that? Do it again and do it properly this time."

Now I had been in her class for months and she should have known damn well why I had had to recite it *my way*. It was the *only* way I could do it. Half way through my struggle to get it out *her way*, she lost patience and said I could recite it to her after school. I was being punished by the enemy. Teachers saw that for me speaking was an exhausting, nerve-wracking, embarrassing process, yet they still hammered away at me.

Tim Newark interviewed veteran British journalist, author and screen-writer Ray Connolly, another stammerer, who described how one of his teachers actually mimicked and mocked him in front of a class to give the other kids a laugh. My teachers never went that far. They were satisfied with simply leaving me to humiliate myself by not giving me the break I thought I deserved. But Connolly complained. Complained, mind you, that his teachers didn't ask questions of people who stammered "because it was too boring to have to wait for an answer."

Tim's book is a perfect example of one of my recurring themes: no two stammerers are alike. Connolly complains that teachers ignored him and my life was hell because they didn't. I'm sure that some of the teachers meant well and thought they were helping me face up to life. Perhaps they unwittingly thought they were helping me to avoid avoidance. But they were making me stammer worse. The more I stammered the worse I stammered.

Throughout my adult life people have asked me: "Why in hell did a stammerer like you become a journalist?"

One editor, in turning me down for a job, noted my stammer and said a reporter must be a walking question-mark. He was right. Sometimes the most innocuous question can bring a reporter a good story he wasn't expecting. When I was working on the Portsmouth, Virginia Times-Herald, one of my jobs was the tedious task of collecting the results of the dozens of amateur baseball games played on summer Saturdays. The scores were phoned in by league officials. One day one of them was reading out the scores to me and said that one of the games had been cancelled. I really didn't care why, but he seemed to want me to ask him why. OK, I finally bit, why?

"Because all nine members of the team got married today."

That little question got me a nice bold-faced story and my first page-one byline. But the question still stands…*why* did I become a journalist? The answer is that I had little choice. I couldn't talk so I had to write. In the hope of showing my teachers that I had at least an average IQ, I wrote a story for the school newspaper, called "Me and my Dog". I knew it was bad grammar but it was in the vernacular, and that's how we spoke in Savannah.

Allowing me no poetic license and making me correct it to "My Dog and I", an English teacher, who served as editor of the paper, allowed me to go into print for the first time, when I was 13. A momentous occasion. For me, anyway.

CHAPTER EIGHT

But there was always the church. Nobody had to speak alone there except the minister. If everybody else was saying the Lord's Prayer, I could recite it along with them with no problem. Hymns were easy. I could always sing, even on my own, without stammering. I thrived in church. I became president of the Young Peoples' Society. I was an acolyte and a crucifer. Open the doors of Christ Church, Savannah, and I was there. I could speak in unison with other people and I could sing. Therefore nothing was wrong with my speech mechanism. So why did I stammer? Many years later, at the City Lit, I was to learn that after a very young age, it doesn't matter a damn why. It's what you can do about it that counts. And I found much later in life that you *can* do something about it. Something besides curse and struggle.

Savannah was a good town. It was cool in winter, warm in spring and very hot in summer. Palmettos lined Victory Drive and the azaleas bloomed gorgeously in the spring. Christ Church sits opposite Johnson Square, one of a series of parks that leap-frogged the intersections down Bull Street, which divides East and West Savannah. Savannah is renowned for its squares; they were shady, almost dark and provided a cool respite from the city's blazing sun. Living was easy in Savannah.

And the niggers knew their place

I was born there in 1932. My father was a graduate of the University of Virginia, where he majored in law and drinking. He joined a law firm in Savannah, married a beautiful woman from Norfolk, Virginia, called Ruth Lacy and they produced me. But it was during the Depression and few people could afford lawyers. So my father gave up practising

24

law and went to work for the Federal Land Bank in Columbia, South Carolina. Crushingly for him, his lawyer friends who stuck it out in Savannah during the lean times became rich a few years later. We moved to Columbia when I was less than a year old. I don't remember much about it, probably because there isn't much about it to remember. Our first house was in Santee Avenue, a quiet tree-lined street near a suburban shopping area called Five Points.

There's one incident I do remember vividly. One day when I was about five years old, I was strolling lackadaisically from Santee Avenue to Five Points. I was, and am, a day-dreamer. I was walking along a street, obviously pondering things a million miles away, when suddenly there was the shattering hoot of a car horn in the otherwise silent street. I remember the shock to my system of that blast on the hooter until this day. I could say I jumped a foot, my heart skipped a beat or that my heart stopped. I'm sure they're all true. Suddenly cold and clammy, I leaned against the side of an ice cream shop and shook.

When I had partially recovered, I turned and looked at a black woman in a parked car laughing her head off. She had observed my day-dreaming frame of mind and decided to have a little joke. My dirty look didn't stop her laughter. I went home and told my father what happened. I asked him if there wasn't a law against niggers blowing their horns and scaring young white boys. He said there wasn't, not even in the good State of South Carolina in 1937. His tone of voice, though, implied there should be such a law and such a loophole should be plugged. Such was the Deep South in for so many years before the Civil Rights movement.

Colombia summers, like Savannah's were scorchers and I wore shoes only to Sunday school. A statue of a Minuteman dominated the acres of lawns in the State House grounds, the capital's outstanding beauty spot. Heroes of the American Revolution, it took the Minutemen only a minute to abandon their ploughs, grab their muskets, and run to greet the advancing British Redcoats – usually after someone like Paul Revere had ridden through the town on horseback raising the alarm. It was a great day out for kids when we would take a bus to the State House and climb up the Minuteman's legs, over his musket and try to reach his hat before the police chased us away. We would then play Americans against the Brits on the lawns. After the war broke out we soon changed the game to British Commandos and the RAF against the Germans.

I mention little scenes like this to show that living in the South was good. Good for most white folks. And, it must be said, in many people's view, for most blacks. I could see though that they got a rough time from the police, lived mainly in substandard housing and sometimes I saw little black boys would get beaten up by big white boys. But relations between black and white were generally friendly, many whites thought, so why piss in our own lemonade?? But sometimes mentally disturbed racists would burn down a black peoples' church and there were even deaths. This prejudice and racism depressed and angered me even before my teens. I had a softer relationship with colour and a stronger sense of justice than my friends who accused me of defending the rights of blacks just for the hell of it. I did it without stammering, too. My speech flowed, much easier against a cause I thought was wrong than it did when I tried to buy a bus ticket. My views, for the most part seem pretty smug now. But this was in the late 'forties and believe it or not, my opinion were pretty radical. My mother sympathized with me but did nothing about it. My younger sister Carol eventually came around but my father and my brother Lacy who was also younger than me, upheld Southern traditions. The closest they ever got to active service was to fire off telegrams to the Supreme Court when the Justices started putting legal skids under segregation.

We lived for nine years in Colombia and then moved back to Savannah, where my father worked in another bank, dealing with peoples' wills. My parents had plenty of friends there, and all our friends in the law business were the upper crust of Savannah society. They had big houses, big cars and big boats. We moved into the second floor of a roughly converted warehouse on Bay Street, right on the Savannah River. The city of Savannah starts at Bay Street and moves south. With the exception of a few houses in the Old Town, the further south you lived the more prestigious your address. We joined Christ Church, where all our friends went. It was 1942 and Savannah, a major port, was crowded with serviceman and women and shipyard workers. Every other person in the streets seemed to be a welder or a soldier, sailor or an airman.

When I say "we" joined Christ Church, I mean my mother, Lacy, Carol and I joined it. Lacy was five years younger than me and Carol was six years younger. My father was not a churchgoing person. I remember seeing him in church only once. My mother was the leading alto in the choir and he felt obliged to put in at least one appearance. When people asked my father his religion, he would say: "I'm a Pedestrian."

My mother stammered almost as bad as I did and shared my fear and hatred of the telephone. But I had no mercy on her. I forced her to make telephone calls for me. I made her call strangers to ask if their children would like to come out and play. I watched her struggle through the calls. I watched the expression on her face when they hung up on her. But usually she would make me leave the room when she made the calls. Years later, after she was dead, my father told me that one of the parents told her they didn't want their children playing with the child of someone who obviously was deranged. My mother was far from deranged. She had an excellent education and a beautiful singing voice. Once a year the Christ Church choir performed "The Messiah" and she charmed the crowd. She became one of the most respected and well-liked women in Savannah and when she died she was given one of the longest and most prominent obituaries ever run in the Savannah Morning News. But she did not run with any crowd. The rich wives all had their own Buicks, but she wouldn't have joined the "Buick Club" even if we had had a car. She liked the members of the "club" and they liked her. But she stuck to one or two close friends and did not attempt to meet new ones.

I realised later that this was because she stammered and did not want to face the ordeal of being in a group of talkative people, and I knew how she felt. I still feel that way today, a hangover from fifty-five years of tortuous stammering. But I became a leading light of the younger church-going set. I had a lot of friends in church. At that time I thought

27

I was a religious person but I suspect that if I was, I was one of the very few in Christ Church. It was a place to be seen to go as far as most of its members were concerned. To keep up with my other church-going friends I had to get various part-time jobs because pocket money was in short supply in my family. They weren't "talking jobs" of course. Along with a newspaper round, I mowed lawns, painted boats and put together Christmas decorations for department stores.

Along with Charleston, South Carolina - about 100 miles to the north - Savannah is one of the most beautiful cities in the United States. The old town, where we first lived on our return to Savannah, was full of palmetto trees, small parks and historic buildings. We loved the flat on Bay Street. We had a small balcony overlooking the river, down which the newly built Liberty Ships headed for the open sea and joined wartime convoys to Britain. Sometimes my family would go to Savannah Beach and once we saw orange flashes out to sea as German U-boats attacked a convoy. The horror of that did not disturb me because at my tender age war was a game. But I was upset by the thought that a German submarine captain could be observing me through his periscope

I was about ten or eleven when my parents decided to seek help for my stammering. My marks in school were getting worse and my fear and hatred of the telephone, school, teachers and some of my fellow pupils, was making their lives as miserable as mine. My father was also worried about my need for solitude. I would regularly spend some time on my own when the other kids were out playing. My mother understood this, she said, because she needed some time alone every day.

But, they agreed, they sensed an inner anger in me and I also was turning into a cynic. Now, being the World's Worst Stammerer, as I have been called more than once, I was a challenge to any nickel and dime psychology. A pair of young women apparently heard me stammer and conned my parents into feeding me and my psyche into their care. I have forgotten what their nominal racket was, but, even at that tender age, I quickly saw they didn't know anything about stammerers. At my first session, they asked me questions like could I read adequately, could I count, did I know whether I got the right change when I bought something? I put up with this shit for a week or two and then decided I would rather play baseball and see my friends in my free time than being asked if I had a functioning brain.

I wasn't a genius and I could hardly speak, but I could think. God save us from amateurs, however well-meaning they might be. These two women were the first to join what was to become a fifty-year-long queue of well-meaning but uninformed "therapists" or outright charlatans who raised my hopes of a "cure", collected my money and let me down. None of them, until I was approaching the age of sixty, helped my stammering and most of them even made it worse.

But despite my cynicism, wariness and cunning, I had some good friends in my high-school days. There was Julian Kelly, tall, dark and handsome and soft of speech. Richard Corbin, the son of an old friend of my mother's parents. We were acolytes at Christ Church and when we were older, we prowled the bars of Savannah Beach together. There was Raymond Wood, whose father was pastor of a Lutheran church. But that didn't stop him from joining Julian and Raymond and me in our crawls around Savannah Beach. And Henry Powell, who had a basketball court in his back yard. There was a wooden fence directly behind the backboard and if you didn't pull up in time after a running hook-shot, you smacked into it. There was lots of blood spilled on Henry's fence and when visitors came by, us regulars would proudly identify our blood stains to them. Twenty-odd years later, when I was posted to Washington for Reuters, I found that Henry lived just a few miles away. But I didn't telephone him because I was afraid his wife, whom I didn't know, might answer and hang up when I stammered. Alexander Graham Bell even came between old friends. Another Savannah friend was Jimmy Garmer, who went to the Citadel in Charleston, joined the air force and was killed in a plane crash at the age of about 22. I was working at the International News Service in New York and saw the story come in over the wire.

Julian and Richard soon went to boarding school up North and I saw them only in the summers. Ah the heavenly summers; no school, plenty of sunshine, the beach only eighteen miles away. We still had no car but my friends did, and anyway, it was only a short bus ride to their summer houses at Savannah Beach. I was a middling athlete and played all the usual sports to a fair degree. But swimming was my favourite. But come September when school began, life became a misery once more. I simply refused to participate in any class work that involved speaking. I soon got a reputation with the teachers as being lazy.

One exception was a history teacher, John Langford. He was short, bespectacled, his clothes were wrinkled and sometimes his socks didn't match. But he knew his history and knew how to teach it. And he was kind. At his suggestion, we reached an agreement that I would do more written work than the rest of the class in order not to have to answer questions or speak. I was top of my class in history. Mr Langford also unwittingly helped me out of a tight stammering spot once. My English literature class was reading Hamlet aloud one day and I had been assigned the part of Laertes. Laertes! I wanted to play the part of dead Yorick or at least some tiny silent walk-on part, but Laertes was a crucial role, with plenty of dialogue.

Now avoiding situations like this takes all a stammerer's cunning. I couldn't plead unpreparedness, because we were reading it from a book. I couldn't simply refuse because it would be insubordinate. What was I to do? I was prepared to do anything except read or recite aloud in class. So I simply skipped the class. In those days they could kick you out of school just for cutting class, so I had to lie to my ally Mr Langford. I went to him and told him that my zipper got stuck while I was in the "boys room" and it took me a long time to fix it and that's why I missed the class. I said I was too embarrassed to tell my English teacher about the zipper incident, and please Mr Langford, would he help? He explained to the teacher and I got off. Alas, poor Laertes. As it happens my English teacher was especially miffed because she had to read all his lines. Then I learned later in the day that the reading of the play would take another two days! I came down with a mysterious illness that lasted for forty-eight hours. It should be said, this was an avoidance that I practised only in extreme cases. The trick was to develop an illness that was not serious enough for the doctor to be called but was just bad enough to prevent my mother from sending me to school. I had it down to a tee.

I continued to write occasional stories for the school paper. But when I submitted a story about how much I hated Savannah High School because most of the teachers would not give me a break and let me write instead of speak, it was rejected and I was told not to bother to write any more. One day I sent the Savannah Morning News a story on the activities of the Christ Church Young Peoples society and the editor liked it and asked me to cover more church news for him. I don't remember what the story was and it didn't exactly set the newsroom on fire, but the paper couldn't spare anybody to do routine church news so they hired me. Thus my journalistic career did not start with a bitter, cynical, self-pitying story written for my high school paper, after all.

Some of the teachers would have liked to have me kicked out of school on grounds of laziness. But as long as I was not insubordinate and didn't do things like start fights in the schoolyard and my deportment was adequate, the State of Georgia said they could not get rid of me. I read the books I was supposed to read and I did the maths I was supposed to do the best I could. I even kept up with my Latin class, but when it came to reciting or answering questions, I simply refused, pleading unpreparedness. My grades were appalling.

I decided that people were prejudiced against my mother and me because we stammered. Prejudice, I decided, was a horrible thing.

CHAPTER NINE

Besides unhelpful speech therapists, I have always had to suffer words of wisdom from "helpful" friends or acquaintances, who were not prepared to discuss my problem with me, but knew exactly why I stammered and were happy to hand out snippets of advice:

"Why don't you just take a deep breath before you start to speak?"

"Just think what you want to say and say it."

I knew what I wanted to say and many times I ran out of breath before I could say it. I ran out of breath because I blocked and stammered. I didn't block and stammer because I ran out of breath. But to them it was all so simple. Mind over matter. If you finish this book you will see that it's not a simple matter at all. It may be mind over matter but in most cases I've known, it takes professionals to show you how it's done. And only those professionals who *really* understand.

Underneath that stammer, there are many nasty feelings churning away.

After about a year, we moved from Bay Street further south, to a housing estate built mainly for shipyard workers. There were plenty of kids my age and we played basketball, baseball and football constantly. Then my father became the Southern representative of a New York advertising agency specialising in banks and a few more dollars a month came in. This was when my parents decided to send me to the New York Hospital for Speech Disorders. The therapy may have failed but one of the few things I learned in those three months was that New York, not Savannah, was the place for me.

After realising that many people were prejudiced against my mother and me for something we couldn't help, I began to think about prejudice in general. Who else suffered from prejudice? I asked myself. One obvious group was black people. "Coloured people" was the polite expression in the South then but few people used it. The term was "nigger". A word that today elicits shock and dismay, but back then was part of the day to day vernacular and no whites thought anything of it. There were churches for whites and churches for blacks, schools for whites and schools for blacks, seats on buses for white folks and seats on buses in the rear for black folks. There were rates of pay for white folks and lower rates for blacks.

Once, during the Korean War, I saw a black soldier, his chest bedecked with ribbons, get on the bus in Savannah and make his way towards the rear for a seat. Following him on to the bus was a Chinese man. He sat in the front while the black soldier, who had fought for the USA *against* the Chinese, was forced by the State of Georgia to sit in the back while a Chinese sat with us white folks. I put this to my father, a dyed in the wool southerner. He agreed it seemed unfair.

"But a nigger's a nigger", he told me.

I must add here that my father was a Southern gentleman of the old school in every sense of the word, and he was as kind to blacks as he was to our dog, "V" (for victory) whom he loved dearly, if that makes any sense. I remember him as a wise man - except when it came to money, drink and race.

Why did we prejudge blacks? The ones I knew in Savannah were nice enough people even though they spoke a crude sort of English and had very little money or education. Were they inferior? I knew that there were "good" niggers and "uppity" niggers. But I also knew good white folks and uppity white folks. I decided to think about it. At that time the U.S. Supreme Court ruling was that schools could be racially "separate but equal". One thing I found was that classes in Savannah's coloured schools had about fifty pupils, while classes in Savannah High School had about thirty. This was hardly equal. Later, when I worked at an oil refinery, I found that blacks weren't allowed to join the union and had to settle for what the white members of the union negotiated for them. The white members had been raised in the same fine old tradition that I had been and a black's sweat wasn't worth as much as a white's. Later I realised that what I thought of as the "crude" English of the blacks, was actually enriching the language. We can thank the blacks for such descriptive words and phrases as "laid back", "cool", "mother-fucker", "pad" for apartment and many others. But while they were considered inferior and blatantly and legally discriminated against, black people were rarely physically mistreated in Savannah, although occasionally a group of white thugs would catch a black alone and beat him up. But that was an exception.

The higher the social and intellectual strata of the whites, the better they treated blacks. But it was treating them more like friendly pets or trusted work animals than people. They were okay in their place. But they mustn't get out of line.

I hated it, and I knew it was wrong.

CHAPTER TEN

Christ Church in Savannah is an Episcopal church, the American equivalent to the Church of England. To be a minister in the Episcopal Church required a university degree. There was an Episcopal church in Savannah for black folks. Let's see what a coloured Episcopal minister had to say to our white young folks, I thought. As president of the Young Peoples Society, I wrote to the black Episcopal Church, inviting the minister to speak to our society. Stupidly, I gave the date but forgot to give the time and he turned up late at the meeting. Our white minister was at the meeting and introduced his black counterpart, who apologised for being late and said that Rick Norsworthy hadn't mentioned the time in his letter and that when he telephoned to find out the time, I had failed to return his call. But, of course, I *had* tried to return it but the secretary at his church had hung up on me. Unlike my friend Ted from Mississippi, I stammered when I talked to "niggers". Another enemy, thanks to Alexander Graham Bell!

I try not to be prejudiced. But if a black person hung up on me they were just as much my enemy as a white who hung up. I had enemies of all colours and creeds. Just because I couldn't phone him, he embarrassed me in front of the whole meeting. And all I was trying to do was be a good Christian. Jesus Christ! But we had a big turnout at the meeting and the black minister told us about the young people at his church. He told us that they needed money and we took up a collection. This meant that I had to give up our Sunday night beerdrinking session. D'oh! Having a black man talk to the Young Peoples Society didn't bother the kids, who were all good southerners. In fact they enjoyed it. Very few of us had ever come across an articulate, educated black person in the flesh and we were impressed. I decided to invite him back along with some of the members of his church's Young People's Society.

Now, If you've ever lived south of the Mason-Dixon Line, or even above it, you can skip the next few passages because you just *know* what's going to happen next. I had a pretty good idea, but I didn't realise how close to home the fan would spatter the shit. My father got spattered and I suspect the priest did too, although he never said so.

One of the members of our society was the daughter of the president of a big Savannah bank and she innocently told her father about the black minister. By now my Old Man had left the New York agency and started his own, one-man advertising business with my mother doing the typing and coming up with ideas. This bank president was one of my father's biggest clients, and told him that he wasn't going to have his daughter going to church with niggers. I'm sure my father saw the veiled threat here, but he passed on this information to me matter-of-factly, implying that he didn't care either way. I was well aware that my father didn't give a damn what went on at the church, but I knew that he couldn't afford to lose the bank's business. I decided to ponder it. It didn't take long for word to spread among the adult congregation of Christ Church that a nigger had been speaking to the 'Youn guns' and it was all my doing. The general reaction among adults was anger and astonishment. I was a well-known member of the church and most of the adults liked me. But this was going too far.

The reaction among most of my school friends was, to a certain extent, amused admiration and surprise. To others, though, I was a "nigger lover". But I saw a way to fight at least one kind of prejudice. So to hell with the bank president and, I suppose, to hell with my father, too. I went to our minister and suggested that we have the black minister around again. He listened then hesitated, but sadly I knew what he was, reluctantly, going to say. He was going to tell me that it had pissed off a lot of the congregation, and that people like bank presidents gave a lot of money to Christ Church. I liked our minister and saw his predicament, and I also had to consider my father's business interests. With a heavy heart I pre-empted him and said: "On second thought maybe it's not such a good idea."

I continued to go to Christ church so I could recite prayers and creeds in unison and sing hymns without stammering, but after this episode I was wiser and more cynical and certainly if I ever had been religious, I wasn't now. And I was more determined than ever to leave Savannah, although I basically loved it and still do. Looking back on it over the years I think it might have been a cowardly decision to leave Savannah. Perhaps I should have stayed there and done whatever I could to help the black population. But who was I to take on the likes of bank presidents? Me, who couldn't even argue or reason with them because I couldn't talk. That's what I keep telling myself. After leaving Savannah, my church attendance was limited to weddings, funerals and baptisms.

I dated lots of beautiful girls in Savannah. Sometimes I even kissed them. But the idea that a girl would actually fall for somebody who became a gibbering idiot when speaking under any kind of pressure, real or imagined, simply never occurred to me. The telephone was the big thing in high school days. Boys and girls would spend hours on the phone to each other. Not me. For a date, I would catch the girl in the school corridors. I knew that she knew I stammered because the whole of Savannah High School knew it. So it would come as no surprise to her when I started my speech-related spasms. Even so, some of them would have a hard time suppressing a fit of the giggles. Many times they would be "busy that night".

Tim Newark's book on famous stammerers includes some pages on Lewis Carroll, author of "Alice in Wonderland". Carroll was actually a literary pseudonym for Charles Dodgson. Tim says that Carroll always referred to his stammer as a "hesitation". But Tim provides a quote from a girl acquaintance of Carroll's which not only gives a revealing glimpse of the seriousness of his "hesitation" but also shows the reaction of some young girls to a stammer. She said:

"Now Mr. Dodgson suffered from some impediment in his speech, a sort of stutter, and on this occasion he opened his mouth wide enough for his tongue to be seen wagging up and down, and in addition to this, carried away by the theme of his discourse, he became quite emotional, making me afraid that he would break down in tears. I submit that all this was enough to upset a young schoolgirl's powers of self-control, and I had difficulty in suppressing my giggles."

You said it sister. You spoke for too many Savannah girls whom I waylaid in too many school corridors. Even if the girl turned out not to be "busy", that wasn't the end of the problem. Once I took her out I still was reluctant to phone for subsequent dates. Suppose one of her parents answered? Would they forbid her to go out with me again or simply hang up? Admittedly after I had met their families, and they saw I wasn't a menace to their daughters, it became easier to phone. I went out with lots of girls but I was the only one of my friends in Savannah who never went "steady". I could not believe that beautiful girls who had the choice would rather go out with me than a football player, or somesuch. So I rarely phoned after a first date. Don't ask me why? In fact I went steady with only one girl -- for about eight weeks in New York -- until I came to London at the age of 33 and met Mary and married her within a month.

After escaping from Savannah High School, my first priority was to save some money and head for New York. I got a job in an oil refinery loading tankers.

This was thanks to a friend's father, who was the manager of the refinery. The perfect job. No talking needed, just fill up the trucks. I filled up the trucks for almost a year and saved nearly a thousand bucks. Soon I was back on the West Coast Champion for the fifteen hour journey to New York. Believe it or not the first thing I did after taking a room at the McBurney YMCA on West 23rd street, was to return to the Hospital for Speech Disorders and enrol in evening sessions. I'm sure this was probably for the comfort I knew I would find being in the company of fellow stammerers once a week. My father had arranged a job for me as a "Boy Friday" in the New York headquarters of an advertising agency he did business for in the South. They were nice enough people but paid me only forty dollars a week. I became even more familiar with the streets of Manhattan, delivering letters and advertising copy to banks all over town. But I couldn't even afford the YMCA. So I got a crummy room in a house on Staten Island, where the ten minute ferry ride across New York harbour cost only a nickel and I could walk to work on one end of the ferry line, and to my room on the other.

But I didn't like this crummy room or this nowhere job. I wanted to show people I knew what a typewriter was for.

CHAPTER ELEVEN

After several months at the agency delivering copy, opening the mail and sharpening pencils, I asked one of the vice presidents, who was a friend of my father's, if I could try my hand at writing some copy.

"Not enough experience," he said. I asked if he would read some of my practice copy just to give me some pointers. He told me to sit down opposite his desk. He explained to me that I would never get anywhere in this line of work, because I couldn't deal with clients. He said I should be a printer. "They can take home 200 bucks a week," he told me.

Now I had nothing against 200 bucks a week or printers but I didn't want to *be* one. I thought I could work with the written word for a living and I was going to. Though he was giving me well-meaning, honest advice, I couldn't help the feeling that he was yet another enemy.

The days at the ad agency should have been lonely ones for me but they weren't. I looked up Cousin Peggy Winston from Raleigh, North Carolina, who was living on East 15th Street. Cousin Peggy, four or five years older than me, and her husband Tom, saved my life. Peggy tried to devise a budget for me to get by on my $35 a week, after tax. No matter how we tried, it wouldn't add up. My laundry and my beer simply would not fit into the same budget. One of them had to go. Well, it wasn't it wasn't a tough decision. I washed my own clothes. Peggy lived right around the corner from the speech hospital and I was a frequent visitor to her home. Probably much too frequent.

The people at the advertising agency were all too old to appreciate my company or me theirs. And stammerers rarely seek out new friends. Peggy and Tom and their friends provided me with my only social life at the time. I went out with my fellow stammerers at the clinic for a few beers once a week but never really developed friendships there.

I started looking for another job. There were advertisements for jobs as Boy Fridays in ad agencies at much higher pay than I was getting, but I didn't want to stay in the advertising business, I wanted to be a journalist. But if advertising was the only way I could start, I would start that way. The adverts for jobs always said to phone for an interview. Cursing Alexander Graham Bell, I began shoving a fortune in nickels into telephones every day. Once, during a phone call, I would inhale and then block and then repeat the process, struggling to ask for an interview. One of the responses I got from a switchboard operator was, "My God, a heavy breather!" Click.

Another time I got past the switchboard operator and got an appointment. My shoes were shined and my clothes were pressed and my hair was combed and I was going to get this job. I stammered to a kindly man for about ten minutes. I managed to convey to him that I wanted this job but I didn't want to stay in it forever. I wanted to write copy. He paused and smiled.

"I'll give it to you straight, son, since obviously nobody else has", he began. Nobody? Did he say nobody? He must mean everybody

"You've got the job as a messenger and you should thank me for it", he continued. "But you will never write copy. You will never come into contact with any of our clients except to hand their receptionist some copy proofs. Copy-writers have to exchange ideas with the clients."

The enemies were piling up. This one a kindly, straightforward man who thought he was doing me a favour by being honest and up-front. I told him I could start as his Boy Friday after working out my two-week notice in my present job. As I walked out into the street, the old familiar question came into my mind, "Do I have to take this shit?"

Normally, the answer was affirmative, but not this time I told myself. I found an evil looking telephone and tried to call him to say on second thoughts, no thanks. Of course I stammered and only a growl emerged when the switchboard operator answered. So she hung up. I spent another three nickels trying to talk to her and gave up. In a way I was proud of myself, I had actually decided not to take a job that was offered to me. So I wrote to the good, kind, honest bastard and told him. But I decided to quit my present job anyway.

When I told my father's friend I was leaving his agency in hope of finding a job where I had some future, he sat me down and gave me a fatherly talk.

"Find a trade," he said. "Once you learn to face reality, life will be a lot easier."

Refusing to face reality or find a trade, I quit the job. Soon after I left the ad agency a fellow stammerer at the clinic told me he worked on a sight-seeing boat that cruised around Manhattan and there was a vacancy. It wasn't a path to the writing craft but it paid sixty-six dollars a week, a fortune in my world. I got the job and that summer I lived well in New York. I cruised around Manhattan and had enough money for laundry *and* beer. It was a pleasant job, working on the boat selling guide books, soft drinks, beer, hot dogs, ham sandwiches and souvenirs and best of all I rarely had to speak to customers. They handed me money and I handed them change.

On the boat, I made a friend named Dale Monroe, from Indianapolis, who was out to make it on Broadway as a singer and dancer. Dale was "between jobs", and gave me the spiel as we sailed around Manhattan. He invited me to share his apartment on the sixth floor of a building on East 78th street, which had no lift, but cost me only twenty dollars a month plus utilities. He was tall and handsome and girls were no problem for him, whether he had money or not. He was a very friendly, outgoing, likeable freeloader. There were plenty of rich people in New York who enjoyed entertaining handsome actors, actresses, artists and authors. Some successful and others on their way up, like Dale. He seemed to know them all and was happy to get me on this gravy train by saying I was a budding author.

One of these friends was a woman who wrote radio soap operas and made a fortune at it. Every night was open house for New York's Beautiful

People and would-be beauties. Dale introduced me to her and I became a regular visitor (freeloader) to her house. Plenty of free food and drink. And there I met Marge, from Billings, Montana. She was a successful model and one of the most beautiful women I had ever seen. Her picture was on the covers of magazines all over the country. Whoever introduced her to me had forgotten my name. I blocked, twisted and turned, closed both eyes, tapped my left foot, snapped my right finger and looked at the ceiling, and finally, like a rusty saw, rasped out my name after four or five tries. But the more I blocked, blinked and danced, the more she seemed to become attracted to me. The second time we met, she invited me to her apartment for dinner. Who, me?

Despite the fears of having to meet new people at a dinner party, I wasn't going to turn down this invitation. I needn't have feared. It was a candle-light dinner for two. And after dinner, I took Marge Ryan to bed. Or rather she took me to bed and easily and skillfully deprived me of my virginity at the age of twenty-three. It may have taken me a long time but it was worth it. One of the most beautiful women in New York! Needless to say I fell deeply in love with Marge. But when I phoned her the next day, she was busy. And she kept on being busy. A week or so later I saw her at a party with a man who had a terrible, and obviously permanent, limp. I asked somebody who the guy was. "I don't know," he said.

"She has a thing about cripples. She feels sorry for them. She always screws them once to give them a thrill and then drops them."

We were on the 36th floor of an East Side apartment building and, with a feeling of anger and self-pity, I wondered how big a splash I could make on the fashionable pavement below. And I was serious. Marge Ryan only took me to bed because I was a cripple.

When winter came the sight-seeing boat job packed up and I went through another round of job-hunting. The best I could do was a job pushing soap coupons through doors in The Bronx. It paid fifty dollars a week and I could get by on that. But it was a miserable life and I was depressed that at the age of twenty-three, when the rest of my friends had graduated from university and were starting careers, here I was handing out soap coupons and living in what was practically a slum. The Bronx gets mighty cold in the winter and the icy wind blowing down the Grand Concourse started to make me wonder why I wasn't in Savannah instead of trudging the streets with my box of soap coupons. How did Tom and Peggy survive? I would drop by their apartment and hand them my problems with as brave and cheerful face as I could.

The International News Service, the third largest news agency in the country after AP and UP, advertised for a copy boy. The advert said to phone. I didn't bother. I threw down the newspaper and jumped into a taxi, which at most times was a luxury, but this time felt a necessity. Despite my not phoning, the personnel manager, Tom Brislin, agreed to see me and gave me the job on the spot. It involved no telephoning and very little speaking. Just changing rolls on teleprinters, acknowledging telex messages, running out for cups of coffee and, again, walking all over town delivering messages.

It paid forty dollars a week, ten dollars less than I was getting in the soap coupon business, but I didn't care. I had my foot in the door of the newspaper business. Most of the other copy boys also were would-be journalists about my age or a little younger. Many were going to university during the day and working at INS at night or vice versa. I was surprised when I joined Reuters in London years later to find that the messengers there were mostly pensioners earning some extra money. In the U.S. being a copy boy was a common entrance to journalism. I found the people at INS kind and professional. I had no enemies there. The journalists even let me try my hand at writing copy, even though it was against the union rules. I got plenty of copy written particularly during the overnight shift when there would occasionally be slow periods. One of the duty editors, Bernie Bob, sent Tom Brislin a note saying that I had possibilities as a journalist. Somebody recognised that I had possibilities. Bernie Bob was a fluent-speaking friend in a world of enemies.

CHAPTER TWELVE

Tom Brislin called me in and said he had found a speech therapist through a Catholic priest and that INS would pay for me to attend weekly sessions. This "therapist" had obtained the use of a Catholic Church hall in which to hold his sessions in return for treatment for priests who stammered. Priests who stammered? Catholic priests had to have university degrees. How could they have hacked school? How did they think they were going to preach sermons? Anyway, off I went to the church hall, where I encountered my first genuine charlatan in the speech therapy racket. The group consisted of about sixty stammerers. This guy, whose name I have erased from my memory, spotted me as the new boy and told me to come up to the podium and give my name to the group. Group? This wasn't group therapy, it was crowd therapy.

Five minutes later when I had finally identified myself, this guy who billed himself as a "speech therapist" turned to the group at large and smirked. "INS told me he was the World's Worst Stutterer and they were right."

Did I need this shit from a caricature of a used-car salesman who, with an unholy grin on his face, pricked my fragile ego? He was as bad as my worst school teacher. But he had a simple solution to stammering. All I had to do was to start speaking in a high, sing-song voice and come down the scale as I spoke. I knew I could do this and I knew it worked because I had tried it before off my own bat. But I couldn't do it on that podium no matter how hard I tried. Every week I took my turn on the podium and finally on the third or fourth try, I managed to sing out my name. But I wasn't fooled. This was what is known in the stammering

45

game as a 'trick'. By the time he is twenty, any self-respecting stammerer has a bag full of tricks, or crutches. He snaps his fingers in order to get a word out or he taps his foot or he makes a clicking sound in his throat and so on and so on. When a certain trick stops working he finds another one or starts again with the first one he learned. But this wasn't even a useful trick. I couldn't go around singing to people for the rest of my life. Many years later at London's City Lit, I was to learn the difference between 'tricks' and 'techniques'. Techniques can work forever. Tricks don't.

This guy's therapy consisted of *one* trick! I knew that trick and twenty others that would work as well. To cap it all off he would brag that he was the highest paid speech therapist in the country, if not the world. "I make six hundred bucks a week," he would tell us with a big, self-satisfied smile. Then a couple of weeks later when the group had grown, he would tell us it had gone up to $675. It never stopped going up! This was in 1952 mind you, and he was making big bucks, he'd hit the mother lode by using one little worthless trick. I tried to hint to Tom Brislin that INS was wasting its money, but he wouldn't believe me. "Stick at it Rick, If it's good enough for the Catholic Church, it's good enough for you", he would tell me.

Speaking of tricks, one I had that occasionally worked better than others was waving my arms animatedly as I spoke, but sometimes it wasn't always safe. In London once I was having lunch with the Reuters chief news editor, the late Ian Macdowall. During the lunch I admired a smart suit he was wearing. He told me he had bought it the day before and in his soft, Scottish accent, commented almost bitterly on the price. Seconds later, waving my arms to free a word, I sent a bottle of claret onto his chest and into his lap. The red wine clashed horribly with his tan suit. Chief news editors have been known to fire people for less, but Ian gave only a wry grin. Clearly waving my arms was a trick I'd have to be careful using.

I carried on at this charlatan's speech clinic to please Tom Brislin, and I carried on being a copy boy at INS and I carried on stammering.

One day my father wrote to me about my mother. Ruth had been ill with nephritis for ten years, but he told me that her condition was deteriorating. Nephritis was a lingering and terminal illness, so although this wasn't unexpected he made it clear she was much worse and didn't have long to go. I knew I'd have to leave New York and my job at INS and return to Savannah to be with her.

I was soon back in the deep south, where I got a job in the YMCA teaching basketball and swimming to poor kids. They liked me, I think, but they still laughed when I tried to speak to them. However, they learned to swim and play basketball, so I managed to keep the job. It was summer and my buddy Julian Kelly was home. I had just enough money to lead a good social life and went out three or four evenings a week with Julian and stayed home with my mother, father, Lacy and Carol the other nights. It was during this time in Savannah that I became a real drinker. My stammering, my mother's impending death, my general frustrations with jobs (the local newspaper had none) probably all played a part. Or maybe I'm just a born drinker. Any excuse will do. Julian and I would drive around Savannah in his Buick, bemoaning the fact that we had no dates. I'd have a bottle of gin and would lift it to my lips. "Kiss me baby", I'd say to the bottle, and take a swig.

By this time my father's advertising agency was doing well. We had our own house built on 56th street. He finally bought an old car and then bought an even older one for Lacy and me to share. Eventually, my mother died. My father's ongoing aversion to all things religious meant we held the funeral at home

After a brief mournful period, our social lives gradually returned to normal and along with the Christmas school holidays, came the debutante season. The daughters of my father's rich friends were all "coming out". Savannah's aristocracy take their social life seriously. My dinner jacket did not have one night off for the three-week season. There were lunch parties and cocktail parties followed by full-scale balls at the DeSoto Hotel or a country club in the evenings. We stayed drunk or hung over for three weeks. We would arrive at the house of our date for the evening, obviously the worse for wear, and be offered a drink by their parents while we waited for their daughters. We would go to the ball, where the free drinks flowed and then in the early hours drive to a favourite necking place, usually carrying a bottle. Of course alcohol and cars do not mix and it's a miracle no one was ever hurt. But scars on two palmetto trees lining Victory Drive bore witness to their drunken arguments with Julian's car.

CHAPTER THIRTEEN

Racial prejudice still bugged me. For whites with a liberal bent the word was 'coloured'. The National Association for the Advancement of Colored People (NAACP) which did a great deal for blacks in its day preferred the word 'negro' despite the 'C' in its own name. By the sixties the NAACP, considered by many blacks to be moving too slowly and too peacefully towards emancipation, had lost much of its clout. Throughout my life I have aimed to please. I did not want to stand out. I wanted to be like everybody else and be popular. But I couldn't bring myself to say "nigger", like pretty much everyone else did. And I became just rebellious enough not to use the word. I would say "coloured person" and my friends would either laugh or frown. Once I went even further.

One of my rich friends hired a big boat for a party on the Savannah River. I guess there were forty or fifty Savannah young bloods there, and after a while I found myself looking at my friends and thinking about them. Thinking? These occasions weren't for thinking, they were for drinking! Well, I was thinking *and* drinking. I was thinking that the futures of my friends and me would have little in common. I was in a far corner of the bar on my own, not unusual for me because I often became depressed and frustrated at parties and, fighting self-pity, simply dropped out for a while. Something I still have not quite managed to overcome. Sometimes friends would come and ask me what the matter was. I would tell them I was just having a quiet drink and would rejoin the party later (and why don't you fuck off). Some took it as aloofness. Others soon learned that it was just the way I was and accepted it.

But this time I wasn't feeling sorry for myself, I was observing my friends. And they *were* my friends and if we sever see each other again I'm sure we will still be friends. But they were all either going to be doctors, lawyers or bankers or marry doctors, lawyers or bankers. They were Savannah's elite. Although I liked them as individuals, I wasn't going to be among Savannah's elite. I was going to be a newspaperman, with a cigarette in my mouth, a bottle in my desk drawer and I would wear a hat (with a press card in the band) in the newsroom. I had nothing in common with them as a group and I looked for a way to show it there and then

I spotted a coloured deck hand leaning against the rail at the stern, watching and listening to the chatter of Savannah's Smart set with an expressionless face. I grabbed a bottle of champagne and two glasses and walked over to him and asked him to have a drink with me. Let's just say he was surprised. I don't know if he was more surprised at my stammer or the fact that a white guy had offered him a glass of champagne. It was a bizarre moment and we both knew it. He told me he had been to New York and had lived in Harlem on 118th Street. I vaguely knew the street, because there wasn't a street in Manhattan which I hadn't prowled. I stammered to him and after the usual reaction, he spoke to me for about ten minutes before we noticed the captain scowling his disapproval from the upper deck and he scurried away. That conversation was my gesture of rebellion to Savannah's salubrious society. But it was dark on deck and nobody paid any attention anyway. But somehow I had a hunch my social life in Savannah was over by then, whether I liked it or not.

So it was just as well that my father decided to move to Norfolk, Virginia, where I discovered they drink as much as they do in Savannah. Although I like to blame my drinking, as well as my other faults and failures, on my stammer, perhaps I came by it honestly. My father was a soak. He drank, as I do, both socially and in solitude. Shortly after my mother's death in Savannah, he went on a social and drinking binge. Lacy and Carol bore the brunt of this. They stayed at home while my father would be out on the town for days at a time. He would leave them money, but sometimes he would stay away longer than the money would hold out for and they would have no food in the house and would phone around Savannah to find him. His reply, according to Lacy, was always, "Well, there are eggs and tomatoes in the kitchen." Carol remembers my father reminding them once that there was ham in the kitchen. When he told her that, she was looking bleakly at a naked hambone.

Most men can ponder their relationship with their fathers forever. My father and I, like many other fathers and sons, had a love-hate relationship. I considered him hard to please. I could not discuss my stammer with him, even though he had forked out hard-earned money for treatment. He told me once he was disappointed in me for not going into the army. He wanted me to go to West Point and become a general. Why did he lay that on me out of the blue at the age of twenty? He knew damn well that I wouldn't even join the cadet corps in high school because I couldn't say things like: "All present or accounted for, Sir!". Besides I didn't want to be a soldier. But I did want to please him.

Once when I was about thirteen, the grass in the front yard had reached the height of about a foot. It was my job to keep it cut and my father was obviously waiting to see if I would do it without being told. I remember saying to him, "I'd better cut that grass or we'll get snakes in there."

"We sure will," he agreed, and believe it or not, this response pleased me. He had agreed with something I had said and I was happy about it even though he was just agreeing that I had failed to do something I was supposed to do.

Official records show that a Norsworthy left Plymouth in 1650-something for Virginia and became a land-owner. Most landowners become rich and 17th Century pilgrim was no exception. He begat more Norsworthys and they became rich. But somewhere along the line this ability to coin it did a runner. We had close relatives in Norfolk, which is why my father decided to move there a few months after my mother's death. His Norfolk relatives were able to move in the right circles because they had the name if not the money to go with it. They weren't poor, they just weren't rich. And there were plenty of his University of Virginia drinking buddies there.

When we moved to Norfolk I was about twenty-four and Lacy would have been about seventeen and Carol a year younger. I'm sure they weren't too happy about leaving their friends in Savannah. But I was ready to try a new town. I got a job as assistant sports editor on a newspaper that had just opened in nearby Portsmouth by saying I had experience at INS -I didn't disclose what kind. Journalists with any experience at all worked for the Norfolk newspapers, where they paid decent money. I soon found out there was no sports editor or sports reporter. Just me, the assistant sports editor. I bluffed my way through laying out pages, I covered basketball games and I struggled through telephone calls. But just as soon as I was beginning to get the hang of editing and laying out the sports pages, the paper folded.

I lived on my savings for a few weeks at home in Norfolk, the biggest naval complex in the world. Norfolk lives on the U.S. Navy. My father's friends introduced me to the same kind of social life there as I had escaped from in Savannah. Cocktail parties. But here all the young male socialites were navy officers. Walking in cold to a party, not knowing a soul, a girl would ask me my name. After the contortions were over, the next question, after they recovered from my big, bad block, was inevitably "What ship are you on?". How do you explain to a Norfolk deb that you are not on a ship, not a navy officer, not a university graduate, but a stammering, unemployed newspaperman who had no business being at the party in the first place? The response was a curious and possibly sympathetic smile and a quick retreat towards the nearest lieutenant. I suppose I'm being unfair because I went to only two of these parties.

I lost my driving license in Norfolk. The cops had a quota of traffic tickets to give out every day and did not want to upset the local white population by nabbing them for traffic violations. So they picked on old cars, like mine, assuming anybody who drove an old car was a sailor or a nigger and fair game.

Sailors hated Norfolk and called it "Shit city." That's what I called it, too.

I found a job as a sports reporter on the Newport News, Virginia Times-Herald, a good newspaper that paid a living wage. It was an hour's drive from Norfolk so I made my excuses and left town. But after a few months at the Times-Herald, my grandmother died, leaving me eight thousand dollars. Eight thousand dollars! Off I went to New York and back to INS, still as a copy boy. After a few weeks I became a junior journalist one day a week. It was more a proof-reading exercise than an editor's job, but I was at last classified as a journalist in New York.

I was finally in New York with some money in my pocket! And I was gonna have as good a time as a stammerer could have. I went to the theatre and saw *Oklahoma!, West Side Story. The Pajama Game, Mother Courage, Waiting For Godot* and many others. New York was fun. For Saturday lunch I would go to Lindy's on Broadway and see the Damon Runyon horse-playing characters in the flesh, right out of *Guys And Dolls*. Lunch was five dollars: one dollar for a drink, three dollars for the food and a dollar tip. New Yorkers have a reputation for rudeness and I suppose it's deserved. But you had to have a riposte to their wise-ass insolence. And it had to be spontaneous. Many times when I have to speak spontaneously, the words just pop out easily. I soon learned the New York style of retort.

When I brought my English wife, Mary, to New York in 1965, she was appalled at their rudeness. One day she went to the Empire state Building and asked a porter there where the elevator to the top was. "Can't you read?" he snapped, pointing to a sign. Mary was taken aback. Well the reply to that question is something like: "If I could read would I ask ya?" Both of them would have had a laugh.

Then INS folded. Or at least it "merged" with UP and became the "I" in what is now UPI. Very few of us kept our jobs. I used four hundred dollars of my inheritance and went to Cuba for a holiday. Havana was terrible. Every female between ten and sixty-five seemed to be a whore and every male (including policemen) seemed to be a pimp. So I took a bus to a place called Varadero Beach and lay in the sun and played softball on the beach with some Cuban friends I made. I wasn't surprised to learn that I stammered with the few words of Spanish I picked up.

I swore never to go back to Havana. But several years later a friend of mine in New York got a job there and I went to the airport to see him off. Now unfortunately in my case, an American in those days didn't need a passport or visa to travel to travel to Cuba. The plane was delayed for a couple of hours and my friend and I decided to have a drink. He was one of my closest friends and I hated to see him go. I suppose we had more than one drink because we both woke up on the floor of the "drunk tank" in a slammer in Havana. The airline didn't care how much we had had to drink beforehand or how much we consumed on the plane, as long as we paid. I don't remember buying a plane ticket and can only assume that my friend, inspired by alcoholic generosity and brotherhood had paid for my ticket, if indeed there was one, because I didn't have that much money on me. He lent me the fare back. When I reported back to work my boss at the time expressed anger, incredulity and amusement in equal measure. But it didn't stop me drinking.

After my first trip to Havana, it was back to New York and job-hunting. I still had most of the eight thousand bucks so there was no hurry. Having money meant I could take girls out to dinner. Eating out is not easy for a stammerer. The waiter asks you what you want and you have to tell him. I'd look down the menu for the easiest dish to pronounce and order it. Avoidance played a major part in my life and I was an expert. If one word won't come out, try another one. But the uncaring girls didn't ask me what was the easiest dish on the menu to pronounce and I had to order the dish they *wanted* to eat. The easiest way was to point to the dish on the menu. There are all sorts of horrible situations a stammerer faces every day that fluent speakers handle without even thinking. Ordering a beer, for example. Simple. But some stammerers have problem words and problem letters or syllables. Suppose the letter B is one of yours. You can't say beer. So you have to call it something else. I know, I know, what else can you call a beer? But us stammerers are a cunning lot. Maybe the brand name is easier to pronounce. Or sometimes if you take a running start at the problem word you can brush over it. Instead of saying: "A beer, please," You might say "I'll have a beer please." Or "a glass of beer, please."

Some stammerers are worse than others. And I was the worst. Avoidance tricks like that rarely worked for me. But they were worth trying. If the bar had draught beer, I could point to the pump. I would then be asked if I wanted a small one or a big one. When I came to England, I found that I sometimes had trouble saying "a pint of bitter", but I could say "half of bitter, please,". Of course I never wanted a half a pint, so I pointed to the pump and would then nod when he asked if I wanted a pint. Among friends I spoke much better than among strangers because among strangers I didn't speak at all.

A few weeks after returning from Cuba I got a job on the desk of a good paper, the Bergen Record in Bergen County, New Jersey, one of what they call "bedroom counties" for New York. It was a forty-five minute bus ride from the city. I worked on the city desk from 9 pm to 6 am for four years. I loved it most of the time. The night editor made it clear that I would remain on the desk forever, but I stuck it out because I was learning a lot. The slot men, heads of the desk, were Joe Dougan and then Jim Moran. I learned a lot under Jim. He was a perfectionist and nothing that wasn't good journalism could get past him. Jim and I soon became drinking buddies.

The drinking laws in New Jersey said bars had to close for four hours a day but did not specify which four hours. So when my friends and colleagues knocked off work about six, there was a nearby bar waiting to greet us. But they all had wives to go home to for breakfast. Jim and I stayed in the bar longer than the rest of them but I stayed longer than Jim, who had to go home to see his wife off to work. Then I would go back to my apartment and have a couple more before going to bed.

We worked five and a half nights a week. We'd get off about midnight on Friday night because there were fewer advertisements in Saturday's paper since the stores were closed on Sunday and therefore fewer news columns. I would generally head for New York and stay the weekend at a hotel before returning to Bergen County on Sunday night in time for work. My weekends consisted mostly of a visit to Tom and Peggy and the theatre on Saturday night. Occasionally I had brief flings with girls but my working hours, like my stammer, were not conducive to a good love life.

Then Lael joined The Record as a reporter. Talk about beautiful! It was a few days before she came up and introduced herself to me. I wanted to impress her. Here was a beautiful woman, with a beautiful name, a beautiful smile, legs up to her shoulders and long dark hair. A potential girlfriend who worked the same crazy hours as I did. But I couldn't get my name out. I cranked up my back and shoulder muscles and closed my eyes and rasped "uuuuuuuhhhhhhhhhh" until a colleague took pity and introduced me.

Several weeks later she said she was really angry with me at the time. "You looked so self-confident and efficient up there on the desk. And I wanted to meet you. But when you stuttered you shattered my illusions and I hated you."

We were in bed in her New York apartment when she told me that, so her anger had obviously abated. Our relationship was on and off and often stormy. It began to fade when the storms would break over a professional matter in the newsroom in front of the other staff and we realised we couldn't carry on an affair and have a professional relationship.

One Sunday morning she told me that she had carried on a long conversation with me in my sleep during the night.

"I learned a lot about you last night", she began.

"You mean talked in my sleep?"

"You sure did. You wouldn't shut up."

Now a normal person might react with apprehension or curiosity as to what secrets they had revealed in their slumber. But not me.

"Did I stutter?" I was desperate to know.

"Not once."

I thought long and hard about this. Had Lael stumbled upon a cure? Was the answer to find a pill to make me sleep twenty-four hours a day while remaining alert and carrying on a normal fluent-speaking life?

I never did find out what I told her in my sleep.

CHAPTER FOURTEEN

On the desk at the Record, I got on well with my colleagues and two or three of them became good friends. Besides Jim Moran, there was Joe Murphy and Joe Magovern. A real Irish mafia and none of them would believe that with a name like Norsworthy, I could be half Irish. But my great grandparents were from Dublin. Joe Magovern was a non-drinking alcoholic at the time and one of the few people I have ever met who could routinely clean me out at poker. Stammerers generally make good poker players because we are devious and cunning. But then so are alcoholics. I could make myself understood among my colleagues. And I was good at my job as I had a way with a headline and smoothing out copy. The night editor told me I was good and he kept giving me salary increases. But I wanted the "slot job" at the top of the desk and over the four years I was at the Record two other people got in ahead of me. When I complained and asked why, the night editor told me it was obvious.

It was also obvious that it was time for me to move on. But I was making good money and I bided my time. Then Reuters advertised in the New York Times for editors to come to London to work on their North American Desk. This job had my number on it! A couple of years in London's Fleet Street and I could come back to New York and write my own ticket. Better still, the advert said to apply in writing, no phone calls! I wrote and got an interview. Then I got a second interview, and then a phone call asking how soon could leave for London. Excited didn't cover it. I gave my notice at The Record and two weeks later I was on the Cunard liner Queen Elizabeth, headed for England.

It actually wasn't all that easy getting the Reuters job. The interviewing was handled by Stuart Underhill, one of the big brass in London, and Julian Bates, the editor in New York. When they mentioned my stammer and asked me how it affected my work, I said that because I stammered, I had concentrated on writing and that my stammer was "a blessing in disguise". I don't know which 'I hated saying worse, the cliche or the lie. My favourite modern author, Len Deighton, says any lie worth its salt must be as close to the truth as possible. Well this lie was as far from the truth as possible. "Blessing in disguise?" Jesus!

It was a curse for all to see and hear. But Underhill and Bates went for it and I got the job. The money wasn't very good. It was 1963 and I was thirty-one years old and the pay was thirty-five pounds a week, less than a hundred dollars - my salary at the Record had been a hundred and fifty dollars. English people I met on the ship on the way over told me that my new salary wasn't bad money in England. But England was and is more expensive than the United States and, having spent my $8000 inheritance, and still paying off a huge gambling debt I had incurred on a "sure thing" at the Aqueduct race track in New York, I was constantly broke.

Sometimes I could pick winners, though, even if I couldn't say them. Once I stood at the head of the queue at the ten-dollar window at Aqueduct trying to force out the number of my horse to the clerk, while those behind me muttered about it being almost post time. Finally he waved me aside. He wasn't impolite, just shrugged saying "Sorry buddy". And as (bad) luck would have it, that time my horse (or what should have been my horse) did come in, to the tune of fifteen to one, about a week's pay.

Most of the guys on 'Nordesk' were friendly and after the usual initial surprise on finding a stammering journalist, introduced me to the very convenient quartet of nearby pubs, literally two minutes from the news room on the fourth floor of the Reuters building at 85 Fleet street. I found London a very backward and strange place at first and hated it. The pubs seemed to be rarely open. I would get off a late shift and look for a drink and find them all shut at 11 o'clock. Or I would get off an early shift and find that the pubs had closed at three o'clock. The shops closed for an hour at lunch, just when I wanted to shop. And the restaurant food was tasteless - "meat and two veg". Vegetables were cooked until they were mush. A sandwich contained one transparent slice of meat or cheese. It was during this period that I discovered Indian restaurants and lived mainly on curry. As I have done ever since to a degree, but admittedly English cooking has dramatically improved over the years.

And then when I was trying to find a flat to rent, there were numerous signs saying "Europeans Only". Were they kidding? They didn't want Americans or what? My friends on the desk clued me in: a European was a white person. There it was again. Prejudice. I had read nothing in the American press about racial prejudice in Britain. Yet in the 1960s it was perfectly legal to refuse to rent to a black person.

In the late sixties, when Mary and I had moved to Dulwich, in South London, a very liberal-talking neighbour converted a nearby house into two flats and put them up for rent. At the same time, a West Indian Reuters correspondent was posted to London. He told me he wanted to live in the Dulwich area and could I help. Mary met his wife and him at Dulwich Station and showed them the area and said she knew of a flat for rent. Mary phoned our neighbours and said we had tenants for them. When they found they were black, these liberal folks said no deal. "We'd like to, but we wouldn't be able to rent the other one," was their excuse. I was never more proud of Mary when I heard her thunder over the phone. "But he's a Reuters correspondent!" she tried to reason. I could fill many pages about the pros and cons of having a Reuters correspondent in your house, regardless of colour. But Mary had the right idea.

My boss on Nordesk was Jack Hartzman, one of the true characters of journalism. He was a good boss and clearly a terrific judge of journalistic ability as he promoted me! At the age of about thirty-two I got my first promotion, the job of filing editor on Nordesk, equivalent to the job of "slot man" I had failed to get on The Bergen Record. Jack didn't worry if I stammered or not, as long as Reuters produced a good file for North America. A promotion does wonders for a stammerers' self-confidence, I soon found out.

I think there were eight of us on Nordesk. It was a good bunch and the humour was rich. Jack lived with a French woman and once Mary asked him how long they had lived together.

"Twenty years", Jack's girlfriend replied.

"Why don't you get married?" Mary asked reasonably.

"Because we don't get on," answered Jack.

Like Jack, most of them were Canadians. There was Mark Nichols, who hated England and its drinking laws with a passion and who was best man for Mary and me. Quite soon after meeting him, Mark told me a joke:

A man sitting in a bar turns to a stranger and says: "I just applied for a job I've always wanted and didn't get it."

"What was the job?" asked the stranger.

"A radio announcer"

"How come you didn't get it?"

"Because I'm J-J-J-Jewish.

This questionable joke may or may not produce a chuckle, but in reality it doesn't add up. Most stammerers blame any failure on their speech. It takes an honest stammerer to admit that he may have some other faults that keep him from getting a promotion, getting a girl, getting anything we want but can't get.

Maybe the girls that rejected me would have been "busy" that night anyway. Maybe our would-be radio announcer wouldn't have got the job even if he hadn't stammered. But importantly Mark's joke broke the ice and my stammer was no longer a taboo subject on Nordesk, which helped ease my speech a bit. Years later Mary saw Mark in Toronto, where he was a leading light in Alcoholics Anonymous. It was that kind of desk. And there was his room mate Doug Marshall, who worked for Canadian Press in London. It was at their flat that I met Mary Apps, who was going with Doug. She was beautiful and sang like a bird. One night she and

I sat under a table, for some reason, and discussed folk music, which I loved and she sang. When she and Doug broke up, Mary and I took up together and married a month later. Twenty-eight years later we, as Mary says, "are still hangin' in there."

The wedding must have been one of the shortest on record. It took place at Christ Church in Hastings, on the Sussex coast, which is Mary's home town. I had always dreaded marriage and the main reason was that I would have to repeat words on my own - not in unison as I used to do when I went to Christ Church in Savannah. But we had a talk with the vicar, a Mr Short and he saw (and heard) my problem immediately.

"The marriage ceremony should be a happy occasion, not one you fear," he said. He agreed to ask me questions instead of me having to repeat them after him. He would say "Will you Richard take Mary ..... ", not "repeat after me" and all I had to say was "I will."

I probably could have handled this because once the audience knows what the stammerer is going to say, it's much easier for him to say it. But I wasn't taking any chances. I doubt if Mary realised at the time what she was in for, being the wife of the World's Worst Stammerer.

CHAPTER FIFTEEN

After about four years on Nordesk, I moved to the London reporting bureau of Reuters. There I was in charge of the evening shift from 4-12 pm. A good move and a little more self-confidence began to seep into me. I was finally getting somewhere at the age of about thirty-five. Looking back, that was a time in my life when phone calls and speaking were easier. Maybe it was because Reuters carried a lot of weight and when I opened a telephone conversation by saying "This is Reuters," or "I'm with Reuters" or ""Hello, this is Reuters" (or any combination of those words which came out easier at that particular time) people paid attention. What you picked up from them could be on the desks of some 5,000 newspapers, radio and TV stations around the world within a couple of minutes. I phoned 10 Downing Street, Buckingham Palace, the Foreign Office and nobody hung up once I started talking. And I was talking easier. There were still the occasional silent blocks and Number 10 Downing Street switchboard often would give me the familiar "click", but I really can't explain that relatively good period…then again I can't explain a lot of things about stammering. Best of all it led to another promotion - news editor, United Kingdom and Ireland.

I began working daytime hours under the bureau chief at the time, Peter Mosley. Peter was posted to Houston and he was followed by David Reid and Ian Glenday, a Canadian. This was in 1972 and the IRA was kicking up a fuss again in Northern Ireland. This was our major story and one of our best correspondents, David Rogers, was there. One day in Belfast, a British Army armoured personnel carrier, being used as an ambulance, smashed through a street barricade in the Falls Road area and wrote off a taxi in which he was riding. David was taken to hospital with a broken shoulder and a day or two later I went to Belfast to get him out of the Royal Victoria Hospital and onto a plane home. I had never seen or imagined a place like Belfast, where the people went about their daily business despite the bombs, gunfire, terror and death inflicted on them by a small minority of the population day in and day out. After getting David on the plane, I decided to stay on for a couple of days to keep the story going until we assigned a new correspondent to Northern Ireland. But I got hooked on the story. As Mary likes to say: "Rick went to Belfast for the weekend and came home two years later."

Only a slight exaggeration. But I did become the main Reuters correspondent in Northern Ireland. I was worried. Could I hack being a correspondent on a major story like this, which was a 24- hour-a-day job and the telephone was an essential part of it? Well, I had to hack it. And somehow I did. I was on the phone to the army and police press offices constantly. They were, of course, bemused at first, but since I was Reuters, they put up with me. When I paid my first visit to the army press headquarters in Lisburn, outside Belfast, after a couple of weeks, I was on one of those infrequent fluent kicks. I introduced myself to the chief press officer, who remembered speaking to me over the phone. No mention of stammering. Another press officer walked in and when he found out I was from Reuters, said, "One of your chaps stammers horribly. I can hardly understand him. Can't you find somebody else?"

"That's me" I said. "I mean, I'm the stammerer, not the 'somebody else'." I don't know which one of us was more embarrassed, but the British Army never hung up on me. And Reuters didn't 'find somebody else'.

For me the Northern Ireland story became an addiction. The Catholics and the IRA loved the press (except for the town's Protestant paper) and the Protestants, for the most part, distrusted us.

It was relatively safe for a journalist to walk up the Catholic Falls Road, but we dreaded a walk up the Protestant Shankill Road. The people of Belfast could spot a journalist at a very long range, but photographers and cameramen were even more obvious and I felt sorry for them because there was no way they could fade into the background. On the other hand, I envied them because they didn't have to use the phone. Most of the press was reporting that the Catholic cause was a just one and the Catholics were being denied jobs in the shipyards and elsewhere and were getting a raw deal in many other ways. The Protestants were getting a bad press and they saw this as a threat to the supremacy they had always enjoyed. But on the other hand, the press in general didn't like the IRA's tactics. We didn't like seeing parts of bodies lying around after a bungled bomb attack. It is debatable whether, in the entire two years I was there, the IRA ever *intended* to kill any civilians with their bombs. At that time they were after the army and the police. But their warnings were sometimes late or civilians got in a sniper's line of fire. And there was the sheer stupidity of the IRA blowing up their own city.

My American accent helped me in my contacts with the IRA, but not with the Protestants, who knew that the IRA received money from its American supporters. The people of Belfast, Catholic or Protestant, knew a journalist when they saw one - they seemed to be able to smell us. The people who frightened me the most were the bunches of young Protestant teenagers, male and female, called "Tartan gangs", who roamed the Shankill looking for trouble -- and journalists.

But I took my chances with the Protestants and Reuters got as unbiased a report as I could produce. One day a bomb exploded in the Shankill and I took a taxi to have a look. The explosion had burst a water main and as the taxi turned into the Shankill there were floods of water pouring down the gutters. A bunch of Tartans standing on a corner spotted me as a journalist and began swearing and shaking their fists as we drove past. They scared me and angered the driver, whose religion and political persuasion I didn't know. They were still there and still in a warlike mood when we drove back, and the driver suddenly sped up, swerved towards them and drenched them with muddy water from the gutter. He slumped over his steering wheel, shaking with laughter. He then showed two fingers to the dripping, infuriated youths. I have to admit I found the 'revenge' satisfying but I knew I was a marked man in the Shankill.

Better, and more informed writers than me have described and given their opinions on the situation in Northern Ireland and the only reason I'm going off on what seems to be a tangent here is to get across the stammerer's fear of his stammer -- how it can overshadow the more important things in life -- like protecting his ass. I almost got killed in Northern Ireland a couple of times. Neither involved heroics. But on one of the occasions, my stammer saved my life.

The bombs would start going off about 11am and averaged about three a day. Once there was a car bomb just around the corner from my hotel on Royal Avenue and I walked over to watch it go off. The area around the suspect car was cordoned off and it was obvious there weren't going to be any casualties, so I returned to my hotel, where I was a regular and not subject to security checks. But today there was a substitute security man, who flagged me down as I entered.

"What's your name, sir?" That question again!

Thirty or forty seconds later after I had gone through the giving-my-name routine, I was on my way up to my room. Just as I put my key in the door, the bomb went off. It was a lulu, more than three hundred pounds of gelignite, I learned later, and it blew in the windows of my room. As I opened the door, there, wedged into the inside of it, was an inch-wide, arrow-shaped sliver of glass. It had hit the door at the point my belly button would have been if I hadn't blocked and stammered for the security man.

Another time I was running up a hill in Londonderry after a big Orangemen's march with a gang of Protestant thugs, one of whom had recognised me from the taxi incident in the Shankill, on my tail. At the top of the hill was a Catholic housing estate where I could find protection, but I fell into a barbed wire fence and before the Catholics could pull me up, my back was in shreds and my ribs were bruised by Tartan boots.

Now Reuters pays a pretty good daily allowance and most Reuters journalists can make a small profit when they are off-base. Not me. Now

I'm as afraid of bombs and guns and threatening thugs as the next guy, if not more so. But the hardest and most feared part of my job was phoning my stories back to London. A correspondent can sit down and write his story but if he can't get it to the desk it's not worth a damn. So I paid people to read my copy over the phone to London. I paid hotel desk clerks, barmen and sometimes I just pulled people off the street and asked them if they'd like to make an easy couple of quid. This made a real dent in my budget. There were still times when there was just no one around to phone in my copy and I was forced to do it myself. The copy-takers in London knew me and were sympathetic. But it was torture for both of us and I lived in fear of not being able to find someone to make my calls. This fear took precedence over any form of the violence Northern Ireland had to offer. Sometimes asking a stranger to telephone my copy to London was not a wise thing to do. There were few moderates in Northern Ireland. People saw the troubles as black or white and if they didn't approve of your copy, they might do you some damage. But I would take that chance rather than go through the rigours of speaking over the telephone.

My bank account also suffered because I was unable to make radio broadcasts. Reuters had an audio service then and radio reports were phoned down the line to London. They didn't take long to write or phone in and Reuters paid us extra for doing them. My main problem on arrival was to find somebody who would do my broadcasts. On my second or third day I ran into an American free-lance photographer who could use a few extra pounds a day. His name was Leif Skoogfors and he turned out to be a natural radio man. One of Leif's forebears had arrived in the United States from Sweden with the surname of Jorgensen. He looked in the telephone directory and saw that he would be one of thousands of Jorgensens. So he decided to invent a Swedish-sounding name that would be unique and came up with Skoogfors. I wrote the copy and Leif broadcast it down the telephone and got paid for it. We became good friends and I don't begrudge him the money. But I had a wife and two kids and a mortgage by that time and I needed it. Alexander Graham Bell had struck again – now he owed me money!

In "Not Good At Talking", Tim Newark mentions the late Patrick Campbell, who actually *made* money out of his stammer. He was an established journalist and humourist when he appeared on a television programme and caught the public's attention. He stammered freely and openly and the audiences in the 1960s loved it. I remember wishing I could stammer freely like Campbell could. He occasionally screwed up his eyes, but otherwise, he just let rip. Many fellow journalists expressed disapproval when he began doing TV commercials. But I didn't sneer. He was taking money from the enemy. But despite his fame and success, he wrote in his book "My Life and Times" in 1967: "If I was offered, by some miraculous over-night cure, the opportunity never to stammer again, I'd accept it without hesitation."

Leif turned up every morning at my Belfast hotel at 7.30am like clockwork to make the broadcast. But suppose he hadn't turned up? I would have had to tell London, "sorry, no broadcast today, folks, unless you want me to do it." Laughter all around. But it wouldn't have been funny.

Although I was hooked on the Northern Ireland story, I felt a tremendous relief when, on my occasional breaks, the plane took off from Belfast's Aldergrove Airport. I could feel the tension seeping from me as I hit the overhead "gin and tonic" button, knowing I would soon be home with Mary and the kids. On those flights, the words "gin and tonic" always slipped out easily. Back in London, Lesley Saltmarsh, a neighbour, friend and speech therapist. who dealt with children 's speech problems, began urging me to try therapy again. She finally succeeded and with much cynicism, I went along to a colleague of hers in London. I had only one session because the following day I was told I was being posted to Singapore in one month.

CHAPTER SIXTEEN

Mary wasn't happy about going to Singapore for four years. She had her life in England and a well-paying career as folk singer going. Little did she know that this was going to be the most happy and fascinating four years of her life. I was excited. But I had always avoided (there's that word again) a foreign posting because I would have to have a medical examination and I knew I was especially vulnerable to cancer. I had had cancer all my life, I thought, ever since I had a malignant kidney removed at the age of five. But I didn't want to know. I suppose I am a closet hyprochondriac. I avoid doctors. However I passed with only a faint heart problem. "Give up smoking and it will probably go away," said the specialist from St Bartholomew's Hospital. Well, I didn't stop smoking, but it went away. More importantly, would I stammer in Asia? I'm not that stupid. Of course I would. Anywhere, anytime and for anybody.

But the title of Editor, Asian Services, Singapore. Wow! When Brian Horton, the Editor in Chief of Reuters, told me that was my next job, he injected me with a large dose of confidence. I couldn't have the slot job on the Bergen County Record because I stammered, but I could be editor of Asia for the world's biggest news agency. Why did Brian Horton have enough confidence in me to put me in a relatively senior position, when the night editor of the Bergen Record didn't? But if it weren't for him I might still be on the night desk in Hackensack. That said, a part of me still missed writing for a newspaper. Newspapermen and women see the results of their work after four or five hours or fewer. Agency copy flies into the ether rarely to be seen again

It was 1974 and the Americans had *officially* pulled out of the Vietnam war leaving the communist forces of the north an open goal in their bid for a union with the south. Although the result of the Indo-China war was a foregone conclusion, it rated among the world's top stories and I was the editor nominally responsible for its coverage, although London headquarters kept a sharp eye on it. We had a desk of eight men and a host of correspondents covering Asia. We would send Asian copy to London for worldwide distribution and London would send us copy from the rest of the world for distribution in Asia. I stammered in Singapore and the rest of Asia just as bad as I did in Savannah, New York, Havana, Norfolk, Portsmouth, Newport News and London. But I was entitled to a secretary! The National Health Service should issue every stammerer a secretary.

"Mr Norsworthy would like to speak to Mr Chan".

"Mr Norsworthy would like a table for four tonight

"Mr Norsworthy would like to make an appointment with Mr Ong.

I was relieved of the first and worst hurdle of a phone-call. I didn't have to introduce myself. What a blessing. Nancy Chan performed all these chores that would have made life a worse hell than it already was for a stammerer.

So there I was in my early forties, some 11,000 miles from Savannah, Georgia, with my own office, a secretary and flying around to practically every country in Asia. Why did the British promote me despite my stammering when the Americans wanted me to work dead-end jobs and keep my mouth shut? That question and the U.S. Internal Revenue Service and its unreasoning, bullying, inhuman, computerised demands for money, will probably keep me from ever making the United States my home again. But it is an exciting place and I love it.

Saigon and Phnom Penh fell in the spring of 1975 and the Indo-China war was over. Like many people, I remember the good and bad times during war. Mary spent the closing weeks of the war ferrying Reuters correspondents between Singapore's Paya Lebar airport and the Goodwood Park Hotel and often to our house. Our house was always

74

full of correspondents on their way to Vietnam or on R&R from Saigon. They wanted to play and drink. So we drank and played 'liar dice' and danced. Mary, especially, loved to dance. On one occasion she and my good friend and colleague, Pat Massey were dancing strenuously, flinging each other about the floor. I saw Pat swing Mary so hard that she was positioned horizontally about four feet above the floor. She lost her grip and went flying across the room to land on her coccyx. Her dancing and tennis-playing days were over for a couple of weeks. In Singapore Mary found an outlet for her talents and played her guitar and sang for the British Armed Forces Network and Singapore television. She also worked as a radio presenter for the BFBS, alongside Sarah Kennedy, who later went on to find fame as a c-host of the TV show 'You've Been Framed' and as a BBC2 presenter. Singapore was a good life, and as befits an ex-pat wife Mary also took up tennis, water-skiing and bridge.

Back to London for a year or two and then a posting to Washington, D.C. and a chance to show my kids, Tracey and Adam, the country where their Old Man had grown up. It was a daytime job and a five-day work week and I would have the time to spend with Mary and the children. My two years in Northern Ireland had deprived me of them except during the breaks I spent in London every few weeks. Tracey was now twelve and Adam was eight and I was determined to show them the ways of America. The days in the Washington bureau were long and hard. The capital of the United States of America is a busy place for a journalist. Practically every word spoken by President Carter or practically any Washington official had to be flashed around the world as soon as they were uttered. And they were uttered frequently. Except for a couple of short visits, I had been away from the United States for seventeen years and the workings of the government were strange to me. And it was a struggle.

I discovered a new set of enemies - the desk at U.S headquarters in New York. They hated the Washington Bureau. I was told they were jealous of us because we had the big stories and got the glory while they were nominally our superiors. Glory? There was no glory in my job as

I pored through thousands of words of copy spewed out from several printers from correspondents at the White House, the State Department, Capitol Hill, the Department of Agriculture, the Supreme Court and all the other departments and agencies. The world wanted to know what was going on in Washington and wanted to know it quickly. There was a 'hot line' telephone between the New York desk and the Washington desk and it was a bastard. I stammered over that phone worse than any other phone in the world. It was evil and the person on the other end had no time to be patient.

For the first time in my seventeen years at Reuters I had shouting matches with some of my colleagues. In conditions like that my speech flowed freely and I had no problems making myself understood by my New York colleagues (enemies). I was moved to the evening shift where I had to track down stories from the earlier editions of the Washington Post and the New York Times that Reuters did not have. Checking these stories meant using the phone to call the White House or some senator or congressman. There was no way to avoid these calls, and they would hang up on me more likely than not after hearing "uuuuuuhhhhhh". But I had to keep phoning them back until they listened. Hours of stammering over the phone sapped my energy and I left the office around midnight drained and not all that sober.

Then something good happened. Something good for me, that is. My pal Ron Thomson was sent from London to join me on the night desk. Poor Ron. He shared that shift with me, and like Nordesk in Fleet Street, too much alcohol was close at hand. We were in the National Press Building and a couple of floors up was a bar and a couple of floors down was a liquor shop which sold American wine and vodka in gallon flagons. I unloaded all the phone calls onto him. I would do all I could to help him, but he bore the burden of the night shift. We both hated it. The New York office continued to give us hell.

But I did make friends in New York. Brian Bain was there and when he eventually took over as news editor in Washington we became good friends. Arthur Spiegelman was in New York. Art had worked as a reporter on the Bergen Record in New Jersey when I was on the copydesk there and one day turned up at Reuters in London and asked if there was a job going. There was and I was temporarily in charge of Nordesk and he got it. Hiring Arthur is probably my greatest claim to fame in twenty-eight years at Reuters. Along with Ron Thomson and Pat Massey, he is one of the most beautiful writers in journalism. But on night desk in DC Ron and I suffered and cursed together. We kept the liquor store in business by bringing jugs of wine into the office. We didn't get drunk, but the wine and Ron's dry sense of humour kept us sane.

Now Ron is not tall and is not slim. He has a well-trimmed beard and moustache and, like me, not as much hair as he used to have. He is most definitely not the kind of person you could imagine jumping out of a birthday cake. But a couple of years later, when we were both back in London, he did just that at my fiftieth birthday party. My wife Mary and friends fashioned a cake out of chicken wire and cardboard, dressed Ron in a bikini and made him up like the world's cheapest whore. I was totally unaware of all these goings on and was held in the kitchen while, in the living room, Ron was stuffed into the cake. When he leapt out, the surprise and shock were total. I was told later that the cake was a tight fit and that, during a rehearsal, as Ron inhaled and exhaled, so it expanded and retracted. Ron's wife Mary, ordered: "Ron, stop breathing."

But there were some good times in Washington, too. The Reuters staff threw lots of dinner parties and we played my favourite party game --charades. Boy!, do I love that game! Not a word is spoken and I'm sure a stammerer invented it. Party games, like Trivial Pursuit and other question-and-answer games, were torture especially when I knew the answers, but couldn't say them.

CHAPTER SEVENTEEN

After seventeen years of relative heaven, Reuters had become hell and the New York desk and Washington officialdom were my enemies. I rarely saw my family as they were asleep when I got home and Tracey and Adam had gone to school by the time I got up. Finally the hot line between the New York and Washington offices became too much for me and I knew I had to get back to London. The big bosses in New York were British but they had seen too many Hollywood movies about big, tough, rude American newspaper editors and had become caricatures of them, rarely uttering a polite word to anyone, especially to anyone like me who had a hard time talking back. My speech deteriorated along with my confidence and I had to get back to London.

But Tracey and Adam were having the time of their lives. Plenty of snow in winter and plenty of sun in summer. Adam played American football and soccer and Tracey discovered boys. She hadn't been to a coeducational school since she was very young, and found American teenagers more fun and less stuffy, she said. They weren't afraid to talk about sex and drugs. As a stuffy father, I figured that was as good a reason as any to return to London. And I was drinking so heavily that even I became worried about it. I made the unpopular (with my family) decision to return to London before I went to hell.

But before we went I had to show them Savannah and St Simon's Island, Georgia, where I was a lifeguard in my teens. I had a girlfriend briefly on St Simon's and once the subject of my stammer came up. "I think it's cute," she said.

My family and I headed south for a three-week holiday with my brother, Lacy, on St Simon's. During our stay there we went to Savannah, where we saw Julian, Raymond and Ed. It was terrific. We picked up where we had left off. I was sad to find out that Julian and Raymond were both divorced, but then so many people were by then. Friends are wonderful people, especially when you have so many enemies. But we still didn't talk about my stammer, even though it had deteriorated since they last saw me. I still hadn't learned to open up. And they still didn't know how to open me up or even know that I wanted to be opened up. It was only with my close friends in London that I would one day come clean.

Britain and America are democracies and there is no law against a stammer. It should not be imprisoned as I imprisoned mine. It should be unashamedly free and open. Being 'up front' with your stammer can relieve a lot of the pain. Bringing it out in the open instead of trying to keep it under wraps, works wonders.

Soon after we got back from to Washington from Georgia, I applied to return to London after completing two years of what was supposed to be a six-year tour. Two years of getting hell from New York. And for purely political reasons, they tried to persuade me to stay. I suppose it reflects on the bosses when a relatively senior journalist throws in the towel and says "to hell with this place." But despite their appeals, I went back to London to a job on the features desk. But my stammering had deteriorated to a point where life was still a misery and I found the job tedious. The work was boring, but one thing about most stammerers is that they do not find life itself boring. They are always too busy anticipating, dreading and looking for ways to dodge the next time they have to speak.

Why did I stammer? A psychiatrist in New York told me when I was in my twenties that in order to cure my stammering, I had to find out what caused it in the first place. He said he could treat me for one hour a week at fifty dollars a shot for five years, and he would find out why. Well, I was only earning forty dollars a week and five years seemed like a long time. To hell with that. About thirty years later, at the City Lit in London, I discovered that it didn't matter what caused my stammer. Whatever the reason was, that tiny little kernel of a cause had set in motion a process during which it would feed upon itself and which in turn would feed upon it while it twisted and turned the emotions and grew so fat and mean that it was no longer recognisable or consequential. Or let an expert put it more technically. Van Riper says:

"It is probable that stuttering grows and maintains *itself* largely through differential learning experiences."

As far as my research can tell no respectable speech therapist these days claims to know what causes stammering. My grandmother on my mother's side told me when I was about five years old, "You were such an outgoing and happy child until something happened and you started to stutter and then you clammed up just like that," she said, snapping her fingers. At about the same age, my other grandmother, talking to me about my stammer, told me that "everybody has something they can't do."

"Everybody?" I asked hopefully.

She paused, obviously wondering how she was going to get out of this hole she had dug for herself with the best intentions.

"Well, some people have nervous tics. Other people are mean and nasty, some people are dishonest."

I didn't know anybody with nervous tics. But I did know other kids who were mean and nasty and dishonest. I was crestfallen, but at that age I was still quite willing to trade places with the mean, nasty and dishonest people. After all, nobody laughed at them.

CHAPTER EIGHTEEN

Now back in London I received what sounded like good news. I was moving from the Features Desk to take over a new section called Country Reports. The marketing department had come up with an idea to provide clients with an on-line 'real time' service that would tell businesses, banks, governments and stockbrokers everything they wanted to know about a given country, and the information would be constantly updated. This was a promotion of sorts and I think the idea in the editor's mind was that I wouldn't have to talk, just cull the newswires for the information and update it on the screen. The editor told me that I would spend my time supervising a group of pen-pushers, or the online equivalent. But it didn't work out that way.

We had a staff that ranged from two to eleven, depending how many journalists were available at the time. And since we had mostly a transient population of young journalists passing through the office, I had to constantly explain to each one what it was all about. It was torment for them and me. The service consisted of hundreds of tables of economic indicators, exchange rates, the political situation and profiles of leading personalities in over one hundred countries. It was hard work and I was always on the god-damn phone either to the marketing department or to correspondents asking why the hell they hadn't updated the economic indicators.

On the upside, the marketing department and its healthy budget seemed anxious that I should visit each of the hundred countries involved. And I once again began visiting Reuters overseas bureaus, only to face correspondents pissed off at Country Reports and me for increasing their already unfair workloads. During my years in Singapore and Washington dozens of new journalists had joined Reuters and hadn't heard about this guy named Norsworthy who was the World's Worst Stammerer. Strange looks and blank faces again. But almost as bad was the fact that the service wasn't getting anywhere. The demand on the correspondents was too great.

When you're working as a correspondent in the field for Reuters, you count on a fifty-five-hour week. The marketing people kept demanding more and more information that wasn't part of a correspondent's daily routine and the men and women at the sharp end cursed us and rebelled. It was the old story: not enough resources despite Marketing's free spending approach to Country Reports. We would get the resources when we started making money but we couldn't make any money without resources. After three years of this, the service was turned over to a subsidiary company and timeliness became a relative thing. No one in our section was made redundant. The two other regulars were David Axtell, who liked me despite the fact that I stammered and smoked and Ron Cansdale, who liked to trace people's ancestries and found that a Norsworthy left Plymouth for Virginia in sixteen-something. They both found jobs on another desk.

I must carry some of the can for the transfer of Country Reports. We held endless meetings with the marketing people and I'm not sure I was able to explain to them that they were asking too much of the correspondents. Not that they didn't give me a chance, it's just that it was a hell of a lot easier to nod my head at meetings with strangers than to put up an argument. In my defence, however, whenever a suggestion that was too outrageous came up, I did block, stutter and splutter out my objections. And boy did I write memos, the best way I could communicate my objections to what had gone on at a meeting. But by then it was too late. But what should I do now? Should I carry on working at a desk at Reuters? Or should I, at the age of fifty-eight, look for a new kind of life? They were offering good redundancy packages and with my heart in my mouth, I took one.

CHAPTER NINETEEN

Whilst work had been bumpy ride recently, life at home was significantly buoyed by some wonderful neighbours. Just round the corner were Alan and Mary Thomas. I got to know them when I was in Singapore and they were in Hong Kong, which I visited every couple of months. Alan always reminded me of my friend Julian Kelly in Savannah. He had a soft-spoken wit and was tall and dark. My Mary described him as one of the most attractive men in the world "and he's totally unaware of it." His wife Mary is tall, blonde and beautiful and an outrageous flirt. She also looks after family and friends. Need a job? Ask Mary Thomas. Need an idea for a story? Ask Mary Thomas. Want somebody to keep a party going all night? Invite the Thomases and the Saltmarshes, from just up the road. Lesley Saltmarsh is tall, dark, beautiful and sometimes gives the appearance of being shy. But on occasion she can match her friend Mary Thomas when it comes to flirting. Lesley's husband Bill is also soft-spoken; a big guy with an easy humour and a cherubic face not quite hidden by a full beard.

Our direct next door neighbours in Dulwich were Oliver and Moira Caldicott. Ollie was a distinguished publisher. His language was, to put it politely, constantly "earthy" and frequently he was crotchety. And everyone loved him. He would do anything for anyone at any time of the day or night. When he died he was mourned around the world. Moira, who became a successful author, developed angina while we were in Washington and her doctor said she would have to have heart surgery. I don't think either Ollie or Moira would deny that they were eccentrics.

Moira was deeply involved in spiritualism and the occult. She went to a spiritualistic healer in Bristol and the angina disappeared.

One afternoon Mary Thomas came round and dropped a bombshell, saying she had been diagnosed with multiple sclerosis. She was in some pain, and clearly In the depths of despair over the debilitating illness, and speaking of now having a shortened life in a wheelchair. Moira convinced us to try her faith healer. Mary for her MS, me for my stammer. By this stage Mary was willing to try anything so she and I visited the healer in Bristol.

No need to say I had little faith. He was a kind man of about sixty who examined us with his hands and told us he would ask his spirits to help us. His fee was whatever we wanted to put in his little box. A few days later Mary's doctor examined her and took some more tests. Then he gave her the good news: it was a misdiagnosis. She had not got MS, but an illness with similar symptoms. The disease was painful but not debilitating. No chance of a misdiagnosis for me. And I continued to stammer.

Over the years Lesley, who was also a paediatric speech therapist, had been urging me to have therapy. Mary had as well, but my cynical view of speech therapists, no matter how well meaning and dedicated they were, had not changed since my bruising early experiences. But neither had Lesley's determination, nor Mary's. They were now joined in this application of pressure by Mary Thomas

In my mind I became convinced that Lesley, my Mary and Mary T would hold secret meetings around a bubbling cauldron to plan strategies to wear me down until I agreed to try therapy again. In the end I think I was probably only half-right and eventually Lesley and the two Marys finally brow-beat me into trying the City Lit, and thereby changed my life. Thank heaven for beautiful, strong-willed women.

CHAPTER TWENTY

I entered the City Lit building in Keeley Street and was confronted with scores of people speaking with their hands or just making noises instead of speaking. They were either deaf or had organic speech problems. A reminder that lots of people had it worse than I did. And believe you me there were plenty of times when I needed reminding.

As I entered the interviewing room, I could see that Tom Reid was blind and I assumed that he assumed that I stammered because he was a speech therapist at the City Lit and was there to interview me before I enrolled. It was a pressure situation for me even though I felt I was wasting my time. So I showed Tom, at this initial interview, that he had his work cut out for him. I gave him an earful of grinding grunts and groans to back up the claim on my application form that I was, as you know by now dear reader, the World's Worst Stammerer. I've forgotten his first question, but he probably asked me my name. I think he probably knew my name before he asked, but asked the question just to see if I were telling the truth and I was indeed as bad-a stammerer as my reputation claimed. When I spoke he didn't react with horror or dismay as I assumed he would. His unruffled response made me wish he could have seen my accompanying contortions or my tightly shut eyes, but I've learned since then that he probably picked them up.

Then, finally the "uuuuuuuhhhhhh" and out came my name in more syllables than I cared to count. I doubt if he understood my name when I pronounced it. We carried on a short and (for me, anyway) excruciating conversation. I told him about the other therapists I had seen and how I wished I had all my money and wasted time back. I told him I wanted to know why I stammered. Tom didn't comment on this.

I had signed for a four-week 'intensive' course and the fee was only sixty-four pounds, so the worst that could happen was that I would waste my time. There were nine of us in the group and there were three therapists; Tom, Carolyn Cheasman and Jan Anderson. The first morning was spent playing the kind of games that reminded me of play school.

"Form a line starting with the person who lives furthest from the City Lit," said Jan. I was fairly near the front but not closest.

"Form a line starting with the person who has been to the most countries." This time I was at the front. I had travelled all over the world, seen wars, met royalty and presidents, and here I was reduced to playing kid's games on a grey afternoon in a sparse, bleak classroom in London. Here we were, adults ranging from about twenty-two years old all the way up to me at fifty-nine. What kind of shit was this? At lunchtime, I nearly went home. But fear of Lesley and the two Marys and their bubbling cauldron made me stay.

Thank God I did. As on that first day as I sat listening to my fellow prisoners, I soon realized these other eight people and I knew a lot about each other. We all stammered to some degree. I was the worst, of course. But there was one guy who ran a close second. On first glance we appeared to be a group of perfectly normal people. There were leaders and followers. There was a graphic designer, a secretary, a housewife, a solicitor. But as we all took turns to speak up some stammered away, screwing up their eyes and repeating the first syllables of some words, while others, like me, couldn't even get words out without the painful exercises and contortions.

I was buying a suit in New York once and while fitting me, the tailor said I had very strong back muscles. When I told a friend of mine this she gently mocked my naivety.

"He was just trying to flatter you to sell you the suit", she said. But I *do* have strong back and shoulder muscles and I'm sure it's because of the contortions and exercises I went through while wrestling with my stammer.

But these games I had sneered at and that had nearly forced me out of the City Lit, served a valuable purpose. We got to know each other more quickly. They brought us closer together in a very short time. We knew each other's names and backgrounds, and when we would break up into groups of two or three for self-help conversations, we learned to trust each other, allow each other to observe and comment on our speech. We told each other off when we strayed from the techniques being taught us, and praised each other when we were staying on course. Constructive criticism, praise and encouragement from other stammerers is available only in group therapy. After only that first morning I began to look forward to the sessions and just entering the City Lit building gave me a warm feeling.

Soon members of the qroup were describing fears and frustrations that were similar to mine. The telephone, of course, was at the top or close to the top of everybody's list. Number two on my hate list was the direct question:

"What's your name?" or "What's your phone number?"

If you get a block on some sounds you are really stuck. You can't avoid them or dodge them, but what eventually comes out may be nothing like you intend. Maybe a bit like ordering pork chops when you really want chicken. Sometimes it can be so bad it literally changes who you are. When I first started at the Bergen Record in New Jersey, a guy on the desk asked me if they called me Richard or Dick. Neither I thought to myself, I'm Rick. But sensing a serious block coming on I decided not to correct him, and having just heard him say the sound 'Dick' it was easier for me to repeat it.

"Dick", I said. And having been Rick all my life up to that point, for four years on The Record I was Dick.

To be fair, names have never been my strong point either. Americans have a reputation for being good at remembering names. Not me. I was always so worried about how I was going to deliver my name, that the other person's name always passed me by completely.

CHAPTER TWENTY-ONE

Once the person you're talking to knows what you're trying to say, it's easier to say it. Most of us don't like people guessing what we're trying to say and saying it for us because nine times out of ten they're wrong. But when they do get it right, then I can repeat it after them with little problem. But please don't try to read our minds. Like me, some in our group had tried other therapy. They were also disappointed. Stammerers have tried everything from hypnotism to acupuncture. I've tried two hypnotists. The first was in New York. He took me to a doctor who gave me an injection to relax me and then started to tell me that I had to relax my body before I spoke and that then I would stop stammering.

And it worked! I stopped stammering - until the injection wore off. I genuinely considered carrying an injection kit around with me but was told it was habit-forming and illegal. Not that either of these facts bothered me, but they bothered the doctor. Another time Mary and I went to a hypnotist in South London to see if he could make us stop smoking. It worked on Mary for about a week, I think. It took a massive, near-fatal asthma attack to make her give up smoking permanently. But this hypnotist, like many counsellors or therapists, saw me as a challenge and said he could cure me. Mary insisted that I go. So once a week for several weeks he would make me hyper-ventilate for about ten minutes, which gave me some kind of a buzz and left me in a very relaxed state of mind. He would then, in so many words, tell me to stay that way and I wouldn't stammer.

And it worked! It worked until I paid him twenty quid and left his office. He told me to think of situations when I didn't stammer and ask myself why I didn't stammer on those occasions. I told him that the only time I didn't stammer was when I talked in my sleep.

The City Lit was different. The main technique there is called 'Block Modification', the aim of which is to teach the stammerer to stammer more fluently. I learned to change and modify my speech pattern by bypassing the silent, struggle of blocking and the subsequent "uuuuuhhhhh". We did this by exploring and analysing the behaviour that went along with our particular type of stammer. Eye contact was crucial. Failure to maintain it with the person we were speaking to is a universal accompaniment to stammering and we told each other when we had lost it. It wasn't easy, imagine trying to look somebody in the eye when you feel you're making a fool of yourself. We also went through what the therapists called 'desensitisation', where we toughened ourselves to the reaction of those non-stammerers I still called our 'enemies'. And we learned from talking to strangers in the street that perhaps sometimes the reactions weren't as negative as we had feared. Now who was being prejudiced?

But we talked to adults, and I wondered what children's reactions would have been. When it comes to having a good laugh at a stammerer, kids have always come tops. Two of the worst times of my life were during my teens and during my children's teens. I often wonder how badly did I embarrass them in front of their friends? Very badly, I'm sure.

"You must always introduce your friends to us," Mary told them. She was right of course. But what must their friends have thought when they were confronted with the World's Worst Stammerer? That kept me awake nights. What had they done to deserve a father who embarrassed them in front of their friends like that? Did they warn their friends beforehand? Mary was a big girl when she married me and perhaps had some inkling of what she was in for. Not Tracey and Adam. But they never once mentioned the embarrassment I must have caused them.

CHAPTER TWENTY-TWO

"Speak the speech, I pray you, as I pronounce it to you trippingly on the tongue ... Nor do not saw the air too much with your hands ... but use all gently: for in the very torrent, tempest, and ... whirlwind of passion, you must acquire and beget a temperance, that it may give it smoothness."

Hamlet, Act III, Scene II

It was during the identification phase of the City Lit course that I began to realise the therapists there might at least know a little about what they were doing, and about the people they were dealing with. They gave us a list of all the tricks they knew stammerers used and told us to tick off the ones we practised. They even had a couple that I hadn't tried. I made a mental note to use them in future. But that was before they instilled in me the confidence to avoid avoidance itself, and to forget all the tricks.

Boy! Did they have me measured up. They knew *all* the tricks I had proudly and cunningly learned on my own. If nothing else, I thought, they had done their homework. Here's what they had come up with:

Speech Pattern Checklist

1. How do I avoid stuttering?

I give up when I have difficulty.
I substitute words.
I change the order of words
I pretend to think about what I want to say.
I don't talk.
I try to keep talking without pausing to take a breath
I split words e.g. (break one-syllable into two syllables)
I begin to speak when someone else is talking.
I use fluent asides

2. How do I postpone stuttering?

I pause
I beat around the bush.
I repeat previous words and phrases (running start)
I introduce unnecessary sounds.
I use fluent asides.
I pretend not to hear.
I start over and over until I have a jumble of unintelligible words and sounds.

3. What "starters" do I use?

I introduce unnecessary words, sounds or phrases ("well," "um," "uh", "you know," etc.)
I use some stereotyped movement.
Shift body
Jerk head
Clear throat

Swallow

Blink eyes

Tap foot

Yawn

Snap finger

Finger pressure

Move hand

Move foot

Lick my lips

Click my tongue

Stick out my tongue

I giggle

I change pitch

I think the only two tricks I hadn't used were interrupting people (that's a no-no down home in Georgia) and yawning. What a good way to put your enemy down, I thought at the time: yawn in his face when he speaks to you.

Part of the City Lit's desensitisation process was to send us out on the street to ask strangers what they thought of stammerers. We were surprised by the positive answers we got from the enemy. But, in that kind of situation, how many people will tell you the truth to your face? The nine members of the group interviewed about thirty people in the Covent Garden Area of London and I think that I got the only really negative response. We had drafted several questions to ask. One was "If you were told you were going to meet a stammerer, what kind of person would you expect?"

I put this question to a middle-aged gentleman sitting on a park bench. "Young and scruffy, not like you," was his reply. I was wearing clean jeans and a blue sweater over a white shirt, which I suppose passed for non-scruffy, and my grey hair and wrinkled face betrayed my age. I accepted this reply with a "thank you," but my partner asked him if he thought King George VI was scruffy. No reply.

We also practiced "role-playing". We would form a queue at an imaginary railway station and ask for tickets to somewhere we had a hard time pronouncing. The City Lit had practice telephones on which we could talk to each other. These techniques helped some of the group but they didn't help me. I suppose I was too old and cynical and was sure that this would not work with me in the real world. But, as no two stammerers are alike, it follows that different techniques work with different people.

But the magic words came for me early in the course. They came from Jan Anderson:

"Go for the sound."

Those words will always be emblazoned on my brain. My first reaction was that it seemed too simple. "Don't start to speak in the chest like you do, start to speak in the mouth or the throat like fluent speakers do".

Oh, yeah? Here we go again -- another trick. But I liked Jan, and out of politeness rather than faith, I tried it.

And it worked! But experience and a weary cynicism tempered my excitement. I had been in this situation before. How *long* would it work? Well, it worked after I stepped out of the building and, guess what, working in tandem with psychological therapy (that I will go into a bit later) it has worked for more than a year now. Why the God-damn-Hell hadn't all those therapists throughout my life thought of this instead of making me drop my jaw, twist my tongue, sing my words, relax my muscles, breathe like a baby and hand them money? Why did I have to wait fifty-three years?

I was angry, but excited.

CHAPTER TWENTY-THREE

Many stammerers love to swap stories about their experiences and how they are treated by fluent speakers. I've met a few who compare themselves to blind people and figure that stammerers come off worst. Now this is nonsense and I have never agreed. But they put up an argument. Their theory is that a blind person, say, gets on a bus and the driver immediately knows he's blind and will react accordingly. The driver may wait until the blind person finds a seat before he drives off. He may gladly shout the name of the stop the blind person asks him for. The same consideration and patience probably will be shown in other situations such as railway stations, airports, banks, shops and all those other enemy-filled places. At social occasions as well, the reaction of strangers is likely to be considerate. They can see the person is blind.

But let a stammerer get on a bus and it's a different story. He doesn't look like there is anything wrong with him and the driver isn't expecting anything out of the ordinary. This perfectly normal-looking person begins uttering unintelligible sounds, closing his eyes and going through contortions. How does the driver react? Well, naturally, he's taken aback.

He may be one of the one per cent of the fluent-speaking population who aren't your enemies. But probably not. He's got a schedule to keep and you're holding up the queue behind you.

"Well, tell me where you want to go," he will demand. The pressure becomes worse and you block and twist and turn more. You know the people on the bus are watching you. You are reluctantly, on stage. It may dawn on him then that you're having a hard time talking. But he's busy and the other people behind you in the queue have places to go. He may

94

wave you aside and tell you to wait until the other passengers are aboard. Or he might just keep saying "Well?" until you spit it out or get off the bus. I've done both.

One of the most frightening experiences for a stammerer is a social gathering where he knows no one. Here again the blind person is obviously blind but the stammerer appears normal. Tom Reid and I once had a conversation comparing blindness with stammering. I asked him if he didn't get fed up with stammerers complaining to him about their speech when he was sitting there unable to see. He didn't. At least no more fed up with stammerers than with other blind or otherwise handicapped people who thought they couldn't change or improve their lives.

Tom was born blind and went to a special school for the blind. There are no special schools for stammerers: they have to battle their enemies single-handed. Tom said that, like stammerers, he has emotionally good days and emotionally bad days, and that the blind also avoid situations just like stammerers do. And for Tom, and with stammerers, the truth hurts.

When somebody asks a stammerer, "What's the matter? Can't you talk?" that hurts. Because it's true.

But if they ask, "What's the matter are you stupid or something?" or "What's the matter, don't you know your name?," that causes anger, embarrassment, frustration or, depending on your mood at the time, amusement. Because it's not true.

When Tom was younger, someone said to him: "Your eyes look funny." "That hurt," said Tom. But Tom, like many blind people, uses his other senses to their utmost.

"I can tell a lot about people from the smallest things. Sitting next to someone on a bus, I can tell if they're reading a book or a magazine.

"I can get a pretty good picture of their health from their breathing. Their voice tells me where they're from and possibly their social class. If I just brush by somebody I can get an idea of the quality of their clothes, which might reveal their financial position."

So Tom was not as blind as I had thought.

My answer to stammerers who think they have it tougher than the blind is that Tom will always be blind. His sight won't get worse but on the other hand it won't improve. The way in which he handles his blindness, physically and mentally, may improve but he will never see. Blindness is imposed on people, stammerers have the power to change.

"I know what I'm up against", said Tom. "It's predictable. Stuttering isn't. Stutterers can feel guilty and blame themselves. At least I don't have to do that."

Tom says that when he encounters a stranger, he assumes neutrality on their part. Well I didn't. I know there's going to be a reaction that I can see. I assumed the person was going to be an enemy. Perhaps an unwitting enemy, but nonetheless, an enemy.

Another stammerer once told me that being blind must be similar to being black. She was black herself and said it was a handicap that she was born with and had to live with for the rest of her life. I didn't have an answer to this. She didn't like it but she had to live with it. I told her I'd bet she'd rather be a black stammerer than a white blind woman. She agreed and added:

"Man, I guess the worst thing to be in the world is a blind, black stammerer."

If you are a stammerer and you were told that there was a sure-fire, immediate cure for stammering but it would entail destroying your optic nerves and leaving you blind forever, I think you'd choose sight. I would. One of the many advantages a stammerer has over a blind person is the hope that it will improve. I have wanted to write a book on stammering for many years. But I believe in happy endings, leaving the reader with hope. Until I attended the City Lit, all I could have written about was the daily feeling of anger, hopelessness and frustration many unenlightened stammerers feel they must endure. I wanted to give stammerers hope. It took me a long time but now I can do it.

CHAPTER TWENTY-FOUR

Over the years I have heard many reasons from many people on why I stammer. One of the most common is that my brain works faster than my mouth. And all I have to do is to think about what I'm going to say before I say it and it will come out smoothly. I think this is nonsense. If there's an emergency I can speak as fast as I can think. If I see smoke I can shout "fire!" as quickly as the next person.

Once in the mountains of North Carolina, I was walking and talking with a friend in the woods. I was stammering away to him and I was in the middle of a bad block when I saw a rattlesnake three of four feet away.

"Stand still, Charlie!," I whispered, "there's a rattler." My eyes, brain and mouth worked in perfect coordination. I think that and similar reactions in similar situations put paid to the "think before you speak" theory, in my case anyway. I can't put a finger on when, where or to whom or under what circumstances I will stammer. The exception is that I am fluent in an emergency or when I make an angry retort or curse in anger.

Of course there are pressure situations, like job interviews, when I could pretty well count on making a fool of myself. But generally speaking, stammering is unpredictable. My few fluent periods came unexpectedly. Stammering can be cyclical. Most stammerers say they have good and bad days. I had bad days and horrible days.

The City Lit introduced our therapy group to the late Joseph Sheehan's Iceberg of Stuttering. The theory is that stammering is the tip of an iceberg. Lurking beneath the surface are all the hidden and horrible feelings that that little kernel of a cause has produced and fed upon. Carolyn Cheasman explained the theory to us and asked us to list some of the underlying feelings we all harboured as stammerers. The illustration is a typical iceberg drawn by a group of stammerers. I recognised most of the feelings:

Guilt, embarrassment, anger, tension, frustration, hostility, depression, suicide. I think my main feelings were anger followed by frustration. But each person had their own pet bugaboo. I say yet again, there are no two stammerers alike. I drew my own iceberg and took it home to the privacy of my office (a converted garden shed) at home.

GUILT: Putting my mother, and to a lesser extent, my father through hell. And then there are Mary and the kids, of course, bearing all the burdens that go with having a stammerer in the house. There is also guilt at times when I fear I am not giving my employers or my friends my best shot because of my fear of stammering.

EMBARRASSMENT: That's an obvious one: anybody who feels he is making a fool of himself is likely to feel embarrassed.

ANGER, RAGE and HOSTILITY: You bet! If you had all my enemies, ranging from switchboard operators, bus drivers, school teachers, waiters, bank presidents and speech therapists, you'd have these feelings too. Sometimes all it takes is a minor incident and my anger and rage explode.

FRUSTRATION: That, of course, follows on from all the above. Not being able to freely use man's most common and useful form of communication and being prejudiced against because of it. Having things to say and being-unable or afraid to say them. Frustrated by running up my phone bill because people hang up on me.

TENSION and ANXIETY; These feelings are a way of life, knowing that every day I am going to have to speak.

HELPLESSNESS and DEPRESSION: I feel helpless in certain speaking situations, but not helpless as a person. After all, I support my family, I held down a job. After retirement, a couple of magazines are running my stories. But looking at a telephone automatically brings a feeling of helplessness, and depression naturally followed. But depression and moodiness can strike at the most unexpected times and places - at a dinner party among close friends I will embarrass Mary and probably my hosts and others by heading for a lonely corner. And I don't know why.

FEEL A VICTIM: This is the feeling I fight most. I know that if I allow myself to feel I have been singled out for some reason for this affliction, self-pity will set in and I will become totally helpless. I am a victim of many of my enemies because my speech has let them defeat me. But I do not feel that I am one of life's victims. I realise that compared with most of the world's population, I am lucky.

ABNORMAL: Of course I'm abnormal. I'm one of the one per cent of the population who stammers. And I'm the World's *Worst* Stammerer.

SUICIDAL: I suppose that anybody with an iceberg like a stammerer's would occasionally feel suicidal and I am no different. But suicide lays guilt on family and friends and is not a nice thing to do. But there are times when I consider it.

FEEL PREJUDICED AGAINST: Sure thing: my enemies are predjudiced against me just like they were my mother. But plenty of others are prejudiced against for different reasons. The older I grow, the more I hate prejudice.

THIN-SKINNED, EASILY HURT, AFRAID TO IMPOSE: This isn't on Sheehan's iceberg, but it's on mine. In general, I dislike asking favours (but I'll ask you to make a phone call for me without hesitation). I am always afraid that I'm imposing when I ask favours of someone whom I would gladly do the same favour for. I don't know if this belongs in my iceberg because perhaps I would be the same even if I did not stammer. I want to be Mr Nice Guy, who never gets in anybody's way. This obviously shows not only a lack of confidence in myself, but a lack of confidence in my friends, which is probably worse.

DESPAIR: The only total despair I have felt is about my speech. I have despaired that it would never improve. I've come close to total despair in telephone booths sometimes, running out nickels. I despaired, in my youth, that I would ever get a job as a journalist.

There was some discussion among our group at the City Lit about whether it was a chicken-and-egg situation. Which came first, the anger, fear, shame and frustrations or the stammer? But it was obvious to me that my feelings followed my stammer. I think the stammer starts and these feelings slowly begin to creep into the stammerer when he sees the reaction of the outside world and his enemies therein. The child stammers and sees a look of worry or, in some cases anger, on his parents' faces and thinks he has done something wrong. He feels guilty. He feels shame because he can't help it and feels it is a weakness.

Embarrassment follows. Then anger and frustration because he thinks he can't do anything about it. Hostility towards the child's enemies who laugh at him. Other children are cruel. He may think his teachers are cruel. Most fluent speakers are cruel towards him without meaning to be so. But they are his enemies. Helplessness, depression, despair and rage all come into play over the years and his personality begins to change.

I remember my grandmother telling me what an outgoing, gregarious child I was until …… well, you know.

Where would I be today if I didn't stammer? Certainly not on a Greek island writing a book about it. I have very few complaints about my journalistic career. The money has been more than adequate and I couldn't ask for better friends and colleagues. But I am curious about where I would be now if I hadn't stammered. I am very occasionally bitter, knowing I would have had a better life if I had not stammered. But on the other hand my stammer led me into journalism. What career would I have had if I had breezed through high school and then gone on through university? I couldn't have found a better career.

As Tim Newark says, Somerset Maugham, in his old age, could rightly claim to be the most successful writer alive. Yet he wrote "But I've paid for my success - every bit of it. You must remember that I've paid for it through my stammer.

"I don't ask for much. As a thoroughly second-rate writer there's nothing very much I deserve. But if I hadn't had a stammer I could have been a great man."

I guess it depends on what Maugham meant; by "a great man". If I hadn't stammered, I might or might not have made more money, I might or might not have had more power. I'll never know if money and power would have been my goals or not. But I do know that I wouldn't have had as many hang-ups and I think I would have been a happier, better person. And I certainly wouldn't have had as many "enemies", real or imagined.

But, for stammerers and others, Tim Newark's "Not Good At Talking", is a revealing read, and a challenge to anybody, stammerer or not, who thinks they cannot change their lives for the better. Handicaps can be overcome and success and greatness, no matter what your definition of it, can be achieved.

In an interview Tim asked Sir Lawrence Gowing, the eminent artist and academic, if he thought that stammering had its valuable aspects.

"I think, in the outcome, if one can bear it for the length of time it takes to get on top of it, a stammer is not pure loss.

"It is some loss, especially when you are young, but it is never such a handicap when you are older than it was at school. To a spirited person, in particular, it is not pure loss. The thrust which is displaced from verbalisation goes into all sorts other areas."

Speak for yourself, professor. I'll bow to your knowledge of art, but not to your knowledge of stammerers. We are all different. We don't all "get on top of it" as we grow older. Perhaps I'm not a spirited person, but if I was, any spare spirit and thrust I had was expended on avoiding and getting around or through difficult speaking situations. And although I have been through some relatively fluent periods in my life, my stammer did not improve with age.

Maybe Tim's famous stammerers chose to tackle, not avoid, situations and thereby achieved greatness.

Apparently the average age of a person when he begins to stammer is between five and thirteen. I was five. Why did I start to stammer? I underwent major surgery for the removal of a malignant kidney when I was five. I don't remember a lot about it except the horrible smell of ether.

Maybe that trauma caused my stammer and maybe it didn't. Maybe it was the sharp blast of a car horn and maybe it wasn't. Maybe it was my teachers trying to change my left-handedness and maybe it wasn't. I'd still like to know, but even if I did, I don't think it matters now. All those feelings lying under the iceberg have taken their toll and my stammer has fed on them and they have fed on my stammer and those feelings contribute heavily to the kind of person I am.

As my stammer improves, so I find that I am less frustrated, less angry, less tense.

"Go for the sound." Jan Anderson's words will ring in my ears as long as I live. I just skipped the shoulder and back exercises and stopped grating out the old "uuuuuuuuuhhhhhh" and started with the sound of the word I wanted to say.

On first trying the 'sound' technique I just began to stammer more loosely, but slowly my stammer, and my cynicism of therapists, faded. I was the star of the group and on the last day of the course the other members presented me with a congratulatory card. My eyes were not at their driest as I described the card to Tom Reid without a stumble. For three glorious weeks I was a perfectly fluent speaker. Then the stammer came back. But it was not a fraction as bad as it was before.

Now I don't have to suffer through the long blocks of silence while I go through contortions and make the long, ugly "Uuuuuuhhhhhhhh" grating noise. Occasionally I may start to block but I quickly can regain control. When I stammer I stammer more freely. People who meet me for the first time now may think, "now there goes a stammerer." But they should have heard and seen me before I was brow-beaten by Lesley and the two Marys into going back to therapy. It feels as if I have freed the block from its prison in my chest and exercised my democratic right to stammer freely.

Why is it that women talk you into doing things you should do and men talk you into doing things you shouldn't? OK, that's a sexist generalization, and the truth is that Bill Saltmarsh and Alan Thomas were very supportive. They and Mary and Lesley are the only friends I have spoken openly with about my stammer. This is not knocking my other friends, it's knocking *me*.

Revelation after revelation starts hitting me and I want to attend my new therapy as frequently as a reformed alcoholic may attend every gathering of Alcoholics Anonymous. I stammer more freely. But the most satisfying result is that I have conquered the telephone. I am not afraid of it. I no longer get other people to make calls for me. I make them myself and I make myself understood. Nobody has hung up the phone in my face since the intensive course at the City Lit. Certainly some days are better than others. But on the whole I am about 1000 per cent improved. And I intend to continue attending courses until I have my speech totally under control.

At my age, this may be for the rest of my life. I think a stammerer can be compared roughly to an alcoholic. An alcoholic will always be an alcoholic but he doesn't always have to drink.

CHAPTER TWENTY-FIVE

An intensive course using Block Modification provides the stammerer with a good idea of how to master his stammer and examine the feelings caused by it. Then follow-up therapy using techniques such as those I learned at the City Lit is the answer in my book. Wash it all down with a dose of group therapy, followed by weekly group sessions. I *swear* by group therapy.

During my daydreams, I have often thought of forming a stammerers' community, or even our own country since we form one per cent of the world's population anyway. But there would be a shortage of women since as far as I can estimate, only about two in ten stammerers are female. That wouldn't be much fun. At the New York clinic there were no women in my groups and in London, there may have been two or three in a group of ten. But they seemed to suffer the same hangups as men. But what joy it would have been to have had schoolteachers, bus drivers, policemen, bosses, girls, who not only understood, but actually *shared* my affliction.

Stammerers are scattered around the world and thus have no economic clout as a group. We can't boycott a bus system when the drivers are rude. We can't boycott pubs, shops and supermarket chains for the same reason. There aren't enough of us in one place to hit the enemy where it hurts. And what about research into stammering? Very little money is spent on that. And there are obviously more worthy charities. Many people fear heart disease or cancer and will readily give money to research into those illnesses, and rightly so. But very few people fear becoming stammerers. By the time they're old enough to give to charities, they're either a stammerer or they're not. And cases of people developing a stammer later in life are very rare. So it is doubtful if much help from charities or the government is on the way. London stammerers are lucky to have placed like the City Lit and its group therapy on their doorstep.

The City Lit tells its therapists: "Group cohesion needs to be high. This is based on members relating well to each other, their desire to be part of the group, the level of acceptance, support amongst members. Group norms need to be developed to promote feelings of safety and trust in the group."

Stammerers must be encouraged to look at our inner feelings about ourselves and how other people see us, or at least how we think they see us. Sometimes we're right about the way others feel. But sometimes we're wrong. Proper therapists help us to change. At the City Lit to get us started we were told to vary some aspect of our lives. A guide sheet told us:

"Though we concentrate on changing 'stuttering behaviours', you, if you like, can take a broader view of change. Try eating a different breakfast during this course, dressing differently, or reading a different newspaper. Or better still, think of some small change you would like to make to your routines. Keep the change small, and make sure you can go back on it. If you throw up your job, you may not get another one."

The next day, one of the women came in with a new hair style. One fellow who never wore socks, managed to borrow a pair. I had been wearing a suit and tie to Reuters for many years and had continued to do so on the course. The next morning I put on a pair of jeans and a sweater.

The City Lit calls this technique "variation" and it was a mild and subtle method of showing us that we could change our lives. We could take a chance and look at those horrible feelings under that cold and unwelcoming iceberg and perhaps change them. Then the variation technique was extended to our speech patterns and we were shown that we could change them, too. There is no shock treatment at the City Lit. I read once about a stammerer who had gone to a therapist who beat him up and screamed and shouted at him when he stammered and it had worked. He didn't say for how long. Celia Levy says that some such unorthodox treatments do work on some people. But is such an emotional shock (that probably won't work) worth the risk? I think not. As Celia says, beware of the "two-day cure".

No physical disability forces me to stammer. It is a one-man operation. A stammerer will probably never know why he stammers and he will probably always stammer. But the bottom line is that he can learn to control it and be its master. Many therapists taught controlled breathing as the cure for stammerers. Some fellow stammerers have told me that this works in many cases – again, only for a while, as some stressful situation may bring back all the fears and feelings under the tip of the iceberg that is the stammer itself. Relapse can follow. Stammer. Recover, Relapse, Repeat.

The approach I appreciated was from two angles: one, the examination of the stammerer's deeply-rooted and twisted feelings about himself and two, from a practical angle, teaching the stammerer ways of easing into a tough word or syllable. Note I say easing *into* it not skirting around or over or under it, but *into* it. As the stammerer learns to ease in and out of stammering, he gains confidence and this lessens the need to avoid speaking situations. As I said earlier, the more I blocked and struggled, the less confident I became, and the less confident I became, the more I blocked and struggled.

I was lucky as the The City Lit found the right techniques for me. They worked and reversed this process; the less I stammered, the more confident I became and the more confident I became, the less I stammered. We learned to not avoid the feared sound and we learned not to beat our heads against it. If easing into it fails, we learned to pause and say the word fluently in an easy, forward moving way. They call this "cancellation". Remember, once people know what the stammerer is going to say, it makes it easier for him to say it. And, for me it reinforced the feeling that I could indeed say the word.

Increased speaking fluency can bolster the confidence of anyone. Smoothly repeating a word that I had stammered on without anyone else saying it for me reinforced my new-found knowledge that stammering is something you do, not something that happens to you. The group therapy was the icing on the cake. In a group you get feedback from other stammerers. You feel a responsibility towards other members of the group and they feel a responsibility towards you. You find out what helps them, and try it for yourself. And vice versa. If you're blocking on a word instead of easing into it, they tell you. At the City Lit we watched and helped each other.

CHAPTER TWENTY-SIX

In the spring of 1975 the Khmer Rouge were about to take Phnom Penh and the Viet Cong were pushing towards Saigon in force. I went to Phnom Penh from Singapore to reinforce the Reuters stringer there, Neil Davis. Neil was an Australian freelance television cameraman and correspondent and a legend in his own time. He loved action and considered gambling with death as part of his job. Call it rationalisation, but I had a different perspective. If I got killed or injured I couldn't write my story. A dead correspondent is no good to anybody. No correspondent, no story. But Neil got the best footage and some of the best stories from Phnom Penh. On my second day a rocket landed smack in the middle of an intersection in Phnom Penh. When Neil and I arrived, the carnage was horrific. I had seen the results of bombs in Northern Ireland and thought I was prepared for anything. But I still have nightmares about this scene.

The ambulances arrived the same time Neil and I did and began literally throwing dead and injured alike into their vehicles. Neil and I counted twenty-three dead and many others dying; men, women and children. God knows how many others injured. Other correspondents arrived, took quick notes, shot some quick footage and left. Neil scurried around getting more footage. I looked around and realized we were the only people in the area. Everybody else had made a quick exit. I asked Neil why the ambulancemen had so callously and quickly slung the dead and injured into the ambulances, and why weren't there any police or soldiers around? After an explosion in Northern Ireland the place would be swarming with soldiers and police. Neil explained:

"A few minutes after the Khmer Rouge fire off a rocket, they let go another one in exactly the same place in hopes of hitting the ambulances and soldiers".

Well, I didn't like this one little bit and quickly and fluently told him so. Besides, if we didn't hurry back the other correspondents would get their stories on the wire ahead of us. "We've still got a couple of minutes," said Neil and shot a few more feet. Only seconds after we drove away the second rocket hit. If we had stayed moments longer we would have been killed outright, but Neil got the best pictures and I got the best on-the-spot story. But he wasn't always so lucky. Neil was killed a few years later in Bangkok covering an abortive coup. I'm sure that's the way he wanted to go: caught in a crossfire.

The rocket attack was my worst experience in Phnom Penh. The second- worse involved a 'simple' telephone call outside the gates of the Israeli Embassy.

The ambassador was known among Phnom Penh press corps as a "good source" and a good guy who would talk freely but off the record, to journalists. Fellow journalists told me I could just stop by the embassy and if the ambassador was free he would talk to me. Funnily enough, these fluent-speaking correspondents didn't mention anything about having to use a telephone on arrival. My driver took me to the embassy gate and there, hanging beside it, was the evil egg that Alexander Graham Bell had laid decades before. I stared fearfully at it and it glared back. I picked it up and waited.

"Yes?" Came a voice down the line. And then I started to stammer. And boy did I stammer. Every block and painful exhortation, every mental seizure and vocal gargle came all at once. The person on the other end asked if I was all right. Did I need a doctor? Then he asked me if I could speak English. All the time I was either going through silent blocks or making unintelligible sounds. It was torture, no doubt for both of us. Finally the ambassador himself was called to the phone. Somehow I managed to get through to him that I was an English-speaking journalist in perfect physical health and could I have a few words with him, please.

Eventually satisfied that I was not a mad man or a terrorist, he invited me in, gave me a glass of lime juice and a detailed explanation of how the war was going. He told me the latest cliche going around the embassies in Phnom Penh (what few there were left):

"A month ago, the optimists said Phnom Penh could hold out for months and the pessimists said it could hold out for weeks. Now the optimists say weeks and the pessimists say days." I used that as my intro. He was also well-informed and I got a very successful story out of that interview. Reuters always paid me a fair salary but did they realise what I went through to earn it?

It's fair to say that stammering had made me a pretty cynical person by the time I reached Phnom Penh in 1975. But the cynicism in the Indo-Chinese around me in Phnom Penh was on another level, and it started early. The Khmer Rouge were very near Phnom Penh by this time and if your ears were attuned, you could hear a "click" as a rocket was fired a few hundred yards away. The thing to do was find the nearest cover and dive for it. One evening I was walking the streets of Phnom Penh and it was almost curfew time and there were very few people about. But one of the few passersby obviously heard a click and dived for cover. I didn't waste any time and did the same. I hit the pavement between a parked car and a wall with my hands over my face, I somehow bounced and landed on top of a young girl. After the rocket landed harmlessly a couple of hundred yards away, I looked at her more closely and she appeared to be about twelve years old. I apologised for landing on top of her. She smiled and replied in perfect English, "that's all right. The rocket would have killed you, not me."

And my parents used to worry that *I* was cynical! I wonder if this little girl's parents realised what a cynic the war had turned their child into. It probably was justified since very few English-speaking Cambodians survived the horrific massacre inflicted by the Khmer Rouge on their fellow countrymen. My own fears were so different to this little girl's. She was facing death every day. I was terrified that one of my children would develop a stammer. How would I handle it if they did? Would I make them feel guilty? Would they hate me for handing them a curse?

In 1971 that S-bomb dropped in our household. At bout five years old my daughter Tracey started stammering. "Daddy, I stammer just like you," she said proudly with a smile on her face. Okay. Here it is. How do I handle it? I thought for a moment and said: "Sorry Tracey, but only daddys are allowed to stammer."

"But I want to stammer like you," she pleaded. I wasted no time in going to our family doctor.

"Give her a few weeks. Pretend you aren't worried about it and keep telling her that only daddys can stammer," he told me. "If that doesn't work, we'll get some outside help."

Thankfully it only lasted for a week, once Tracey realised that Daddy didn't want her to stammer. But in many children it's not that easy. Celia Levy says it's important to catch it early and watch what situations the child stammers in. For instance, if parents argue in front of the child, the child may be distressed and try to attract their attention by stammer-talking to them so they will stop arguing. And then when he realises that his stammer has caught the attention of his parents and they stop arguing, he will continue to stammer to keep the peace. How the child stammers is also a pointer to whether it's a temporary one or whether it could develop into a lifelong problem. If the speech pattern is repetition of words such as ball-ball-ball, it may be temporary. But if its b-b-b-ball, it's possible that it could be a serious stammer.

So when to seek outside help? If you are worried, see a therapist and the sooner the better. Once a child reaches the age of about thirteen, Celia says, the family's attitude or whatever caused the stammer, doesn't matter. Catch it early. But what speech therapist? There are probably still plenty of charlatans and snake-oil salesmen about. A good tart would be to consult the Association of Stammerers or the College of Speech and Language Therapy, both in London. The City Lit has courses only for adult stammerers but they will recommend therapists. Do you come clean and tell the child you are taking him to a therapist? Will this add to his hang-up? Celia says the parents should first visit the therapist without the child. If the child and parents have been open with each other about the stammer and the child can discuss it freely with them, the therapist may tell you to give it to him straight.

A grandmother played a part in Tim Newark's story of stammering, too. Tim, whose father stuttered, had uncomprehending parents. They either ignored his stammer, were embarrassed by it or simply told him to "speak properly".

"One day when my father was about thirteen, he was stuttering quite badly to his mother and she responded impatiently:, "For goodness sake, Peter, speak the King's English.".

"And in that rare flash of fluency, often attained by stammerers in highly emotional situations, my father replied: 'I do, don't I? The king stutters.' His patriotic mother, surprised and feeling that the king had been insulted, clipped him round the head."

CHAPTER TWENTY-SEVEN

Having a small, trusted group of people around you is crucial, I think, to a stammerer. Close family and friends can play an invaluable part in providing support an encouragement, even if sometimes you just don't want to talk about it. don't. I was lucky in that my friends, Alan and Mary Thomas and Bill and Lesley Saltmarsh, lived within walking distance in Dulwich. Lesley's the speech therapist and Bill and Alan and I became friends through Reuters. I could always speak to Lesley about it, I felt, because she was a professional. Mary Thomas became a good friend soon after we returned from Asia and she and Alan moved to Dulwich. Lesley was a friend as well as a professional, and she was a friend of Mary and Alan's. So why not talk to them about it, too? Soon I felt free enough to talk to the rest of them about it. Once the air is cleared and the fact that you stammer is brought out into the open, I, for one, feel easier and probably stammer a bit less. I gave them a taste of what it's like to be a stammerer and they empathised. But it wasn't easy and sometimes it took an irritating incident to break the ice; a couple of them would carry on side conversations while I was performing my back exercises and struggling through a silent block. A couple of times I made my displeasure known.

Looking back on it, it was childish to be angry. I remember the breakthrough well. Mary and Alan and my Mary and I were in a pub in Southeast London and while I was going through a block, Mary and Alan started a side conversation. I stopped even trying to speak. When they realised this and asked me to continue, I pouted and said it was so unimportant that I had forgotten what it was. They urged me again, and with a hollow cheerfulness, I insisted that I had forgotten. It was only when I felt guilty about treating my friends this way that I brought the subject of my stammer up. I think it was the next day when I said to Mary Thomas something like:

"Sorry I got pissed off yesterday, but it's so hard to start again." There, It was out in the open. We could talk about it. After that the six of us could and would frequently discuss it. And a sympathetic ear and an encouraging word goes a long way with a stammerer. With understanding friends, we can let out some of the bottled up frustrations and life becomes a little less stressful. If you have a stammering friend, offer him the chance to open up to you. Give him opportunities to bring the subject up. And don't irritate him by coming up with all the old cliches that he has tried before:

"Think what you're going to say."

"Take a deep breath."

"Relax."

Don't ever assume what a stammerer's going to say. And, for God's sake, don't think that you are doing him a favour by not making phone calls for him when he asks you to, or doing the ordering in a restaurant. Help him dodge every speaking situation you sense he wants you to. I was always grateful to family and friends when they stepped in and introduced me to someone or made phone calls for me.

Until, that is, I gained the confidence and learned the techniques to do these things for myself. Mary had spent twenty-eight years making phone calls for me. After I finished the intensive course at the City Lit, she would watch in amazement as I took over much of the household business that had to be done on the telephone. Breaking the ice, even with a stammerer you meet for the first time, might make life easier for him. You might mention his stammer in a casual and friendly way, like: "Have you always stammered?"

Or "I know a stammerer. Have you got any tips for him?" If he's anything like me, he will silently thank you and be as open as he can about it. I don't look back on my life of avoiding difficult speaking situations with any guilt or feeling of weakness. I'm not saying avoidance is a good thing, anymore than sleeping pills are good things -unless you can't get to sleep.

Avoidance was a necessity and I recommend it to all unenlightened stammerers who haven't undergone good therapy, therapy that uses Block Modification or something similar.

If it makes life easier to order pork instead of chicken or pay extra on the underground, cut classes, feign illness then go ahead and do it until you can make your way to somewhere like the City Lit.

Breaking the ice and getting your stammer out in the open can be difficult, but worthwhile. I belonged to a club in Savannah run by the YMCA. It was called Hi-Y and its membership consisted of high-school boys. We held elections every year and I wanted my friend Bill Ross to be treasurer. And I felt that I had to nominate him, which I did on paper. But at the election meeting, the nominator had to give a short speech in favour of his candidate.

The "campaign speech" was limited to two minutes per nominator. I dreaded this but I felt I had to do it for Bill.

This was something even I could not avoid. I got up to speak. I could feel the tension in the room of about forty boys who all knew me. For the record, we had to give our name.

I grated out "IIIIIIII'mmmmmm uuuuuuuhhhhhhh Rrrrrrick uuuuuuhhhhh NNNNNNNNNNNNorswwwwworthy and I have a nnnnnnomnnnnation (long block) to make. But iiiiiitttt wwwwwwilll p-p-prob (long block) -abbbly take me the whole two minutes just to say his name."

The room broke into laughter and cheers, and with the crowd on my side, I spoke relatively fluently for two minutes and Bill Ross won.

So if you have a friend or relative who stammers and wants to avoid speaking situations, then help him. Don't be afraid to gently, and warmly address the elephant in the room.

CHAPTER TWENTY-EIGHT

Leaving Reuters was a traumatic experience. Ninety per cent of my friends were at Reuters. Before I left I did a bit of travelling and it was good to see old mates in Paris, Stockholm, Hong Kong, Rome, Washington. Now it would be over. I threw the traditional leaving party in a room over a pub in Fleet Street. There were about a hundred people there and Peter Gregson, another long time friend, made a flattering and humourous speech and told several anecdotes about my career.

One was about my arrival in Belgrade after an overnight train from Vienna. I was greeted at the station by a sturdy gent who was approaching at least 70 years of age.

"Taxi?" He offered me.

"Yes, please" I replied, relieved that I wouldn't have to carry my heavy luggage.

"Which hotel?"

I told him and he hoisted my heavy suitcase onto his shoulders and headed out of the station, past the taxi rank and across a wide busy street at a pace I had a hard time maintaining even without a suitcase.

"You must have parked your taxi a long way from the station" I said. No reply. We were by now walking up a very steep hill and I was beginning to perspire. No replies to my by now almost desperate pleas for him to tell me where we were going. I figured we were headed for a dark alley where he would relieve me of my money and perhaps my consciousness. Perhaps my life! But no. After another five minutes, he put my bags down in front of my hotel and demanded the equivalent of ten dollars. Breathing heavily, I did not see the funny side of it at that time.

I went inside, followed by my 'driver' and stammered out the story to the desk clerk and other staff. They tried to keep a straight face and failed. About ten onlookers in the small lobby broke into laughter after I had rasped and blocked out my story of this outrageous rip off - it turned out that a taxi would only have cost something over a dollar. With a red face and a sheepish smile I handed my 'taxi' driver' the ten dollars and hurriedly went to my room, amid stifled giggles and laughter from the hotel staff.

A retirement party should be a happy occasion and one to look forward to. I looked forward to it all right -- with trepidation. A speech was required. A retirement speech can last from ten minutes to half an hour. Mine didn't.

By the time Peter turned the floor over to me, a familiar tension had come over the room. Mary and Tracey and Adam were there. Everybody else in this room was my friend.

I was nervous and full of anxiety, knowing I had to speak with everyone's full attention. But then something quite unexpected and wonderful happened. Suddenly a sort of fluency came over me.

"I know what you're all thinking," I said perfectly, and paused. (What they were thinking was: "This is going to be embarrassing for us and for Rick, the poor bastard.)

"You're all thinking I'm going to give one of my long-winded speeches."

Laughter and the ice was broken. My retirement speech, like my wedding, was the shortest on record. But the few words I did say, I said fairly fluently. I told you stammer is unpredictable. A lucky flash of fluency broke the ice and all went well. But during the preceding days, my supply of sleeping pills dwindled considerably. I think one reason why some stammerers occasionally contemplate suicide is the sure and certain knowledge that they will not be required to make a speech at the funeral.

The truth is that for a while now I had been in cahoots with the two Marys. I had asked my Mary and Mary Thomas to tell me when I avoided eye contact or would start to fight a block. They didn't even have to say anything, just point to their eyes or give me a sharp look and then I would remember to use the techniques I had been learning in therapy. My general speech was far from fluent (Tom Reid told me he'd never known a stammerer to be completely cured by therapy) but I did have a spring in my step, and my speech, knowing I had techniques at my disposal that I had confidence in. I was still stammering, but stammering more freely, easing into blocks instead of batting my head (or chest, arms, or back) against them.

One of the more unusual techniques is 'voluntary' stammering; to stammer on purpose when there is no block. It sounds contrary, doesn't it, but the theory is that when you set out to do that which you fear, the fear is likely to decrease dramatically. I've heard that when pianists keep hitting a wrong note, they will intentionally hit it and that stops them from repeating the error. It must be the same principle.

Actual 'modifcation' is a method that teaches a stammerer what to do before, during and after a stammer. It is a direct attack on the tip of the iceberg - the stammer itself:

Cancellation: This involves pausing for two or three seconds after a stammered word and repeating it in an easy, slow-motion, forward moving way, rewarding the stammerer with an easy-going taste of fluency.

In-block correction or pullouts: This is used when a stammer was not anticipated and the stammerer tries to change the course of the block, he aims to release the sound slowly, smoothly and evenly and then to ease forward into the word.

Pre-block correction: This technique is used when the stammerer sees that he is going to block on a word. It takes the form of an ambush in slow motion. He pauses, sneaks up on the word, and then slides into it.

Admittedly, following these techniques is far from easy, especially for someone who has stammered for as long as I have. But I am convinced that if the stammerer is prepared to concentrate on them and practice them until they become second nature, they will work.

Easier written than done. Easier done than said.

CHAPTER TWENTY-NINE

I've said that I can speak quickly and fluently in certain situations, such as when there's a rattlesnake at my feet. I also never stammer when I curse spontaneously – just ask my family and friends. If I curse (or 'cuss' as everyone says in Savannah) out of anger the words leap from my mouth effortlessly. And anger and frustration were always just below the tip of the iceberg.

Once when Tracey was about four years old, we had some fairly strait-laced friends over to dinner and we wanted to show them some photographs that were supposed to be in some dresser upstairs and Mary asked me to get them. Of course they weren't where they were supposed to be and the anger set in. When I had been gone a long time, Mary sent Tracey upstairs to ask what was taking so long. I was frustrated and I told Tracey what the matter was. She returned and startled our guests and embarrassed Mary by saying innocently: "Daddy says he can't find the goddam things."

No stammering is involved in bursts of temper, anger and frustrations. Perhaps I cussed more than I would had I not been a stammerer, knowing they were words that could spill more freely from my lips.

As much a blessing as a secretary is, and the many burdens she carries during a stammerer's working day, her value pales beside that of a stammerer's wife. Mary was well aware that I stammered when we married. But I'm sure she didn't realise that she faced twenty-eight years of making telephone calls for me, handling introductions and dealing with all the speaking situations I simply could not handle. And although she never mentioned it, there was also the embarrassment. No woman likes to see her man make a fool of himself.

While we were in Washington, our landlords wanted to get us out of the house so they could sell it, and came up with some spurious charges against us and sued us for about fourteen hundred dollars. The case went to court. By all rights, it was my job to testify on our behalf. No way Jose. I handed that little ordeal to Mary. She handled it beautifully, but during a break in her testimony, I could see the coffee cup shaking in her hand. Why hadn't I stood up like a man and ploughed through it? Mary won the case. But it was my job and I had avoided it. Avoidance can bring guilt.

But for Mary, I'm sure that having to testify in the court case - which I would now have the confidence to handle - was nothing compared with having to endure all the below-the-surface fears, scars and turmoil that twenty-odd years of stammering had left me. She certainly wasn't prepared for unexpected bouts of moodiness and unexplained bursts of temper that these feelings sometimes produce. Oh yes, and all the cussing.

And I know that my need for privacy hurts her. In order to ease my conscience, I take over the kitchen and banish everyone from it for an hour or so every day and listen to music, drink, daydream and cook supper and Sunday lunch. The need for privacy, the moodiness and temper flashes may never leave me, because I'm sixty years old and they may be too ingrained.

My drinking is another curse, which has made life sometimes unendurable for Mary, and which I like to blame on my stammer or my father. I'm probably too old to stop that as well. All I can say is that I have cut down and I don't embarrass her in public, at least not because of my drinking. And besides, I like to drink and our friends like to drink. The problem is that I drink more than most of them. When we would go to parties, I tagged along behind Mary, letting her do the talking and the introducing while I kept quiet, drank away and appeared aloof. And rude, I was sometimes told, by Mary.

Even today and even among close friends, I can't beat that feeling of sometimes having to drop out of a social occasion and sit alone in a corner brooding, embarrassing Mary, my hosts and cutting off myself from my friends. I even do this at my own parties, where I am supposed to play host.

Maybe the therapists at the New York Hospital for Speech Disorders were right when they told me I was a bum. But they gave me no insight into my personality. The City Lit gave me an iceberg to chip away at and I'm working on it. But despite my stammer and all the problems, practical and emotional, that go with it, Mary has never completely given up on me. But I know that sometimes her lot has not been a happy one.

Recently I've been inspired, and encouraged, to sit back and look at all those feelings under the tip of my personal iceberg. As I write now, the peace and solitude of a Greek Island have given me the opportunity to do so. Ok, so were all these bus drivers, bosses, policemen, Norfolk debs and the New York desk really my enemies?

I've said that I have met only a handful of stammerers outside speech therapy courses. But when I did meet a stammerer, what was MY reaction to them? I can't remember. But I must have come upon them unexpectedly, so there must have been a reaction on my part. What would that reaction have been? I'm sure it wasn't hostility or incomprehensiveness or amusement. But my face must have shown some kind of surprise.

I'm sure I didn't try to get them to open up. I do remember one time when I met a stammerer on an airplane. He opened the conversation and when I stammered right back at him, his reaction was one of surprise and then suspicion. I'm sure he probably thought I was mocking him. So we blocked and stammered away to each other for the entire journey without mentioning the fact that the other stammered. I didn't try to help him and he didn't try to help me break the ice.

Was I his enemy? Was he, a fellow stammerer, my enemy?

I guess we were both our own enemies and each other's. Here was a chance to open up and neither of us took it.

CHAPTER THIRTY

"How light and portable my pain feels now,"

King Lear Act 3, Scene 6

So here on this lonely island, I took the cold plunge and delved below the surface of what had become my *new* iceberg and tried to examine the changes that obviously were taking place. The old fears and doubts had not disappeared, but they were changing, fading even. Even the City Lit can't provide a quick overnight emotional enema to clean out feelings that have been harboured for a lifetime. I conclude that by understanding the rationale and process of therapy, stammerers are encouraged to become *our own* speech therapists. So as I look out on this Greek island, I contemplate the differences between my old iceberg, and my new one.

Do I still feel guilty? Yes. I still feel guilty about the torment I put my mother through, and have confused feelings about what she put me through. But I thought, what if one or both of my children *had* stammered? Wouldn't I have done the same for them? It would have been tortuous, but I would have done it. That's what parents are for, and that realisation eases the guilt. And how about the embarrassment and emotional stress and extra duties (mainly telephone calls) I put Mary and the kids through? My speech is a fraction as bad as it was, so the embarrassment will be less and that's a comfort to them as well as me. perhaps I can make up for it. Perhaps I can't. Perhaps I don't have to.

When I had completed the City Lit intensive course and was speaking 1000 per cent more fluently, Lesley and Bill Saltmarsh, Mary and Alan Thomas and were sitting around a table in a country pub and I was babbling away proudly when Leslie interrupted me to make a point. I must have given her a sharp look. "You see, we can interrupt you now," she said. In the past I might be listening in on an animated conversation my friends were having, interrupting each other, talking over each other until I tried to put my two cents' worth in. My friends would then duly put a sock in it and let me go through my contortions -- putting a damper on the whole conversation. Yes, I feel guilty, or maybe regretful, about that. But I think they will forgive me. After all, they put up with me for long enough.

Am I still embarrassed? Simply put, far less so, as my stammer is far less severe.

What of the anger, the rage, the hostility? The more I realise that stammering is self-imposed, because of whatever long-past reason, the fewer enemies I have and the less angry I become. The less angry I am the less I stammer and the less I stammer the less the rage and hostility. This doesn't mean I don't' get angry or that I am a placid, laid-back person. Perish the thought! It's just that I am less angry at my speech-related enemies.

The frustrations are still there, but they are more or less the same frustrations that fluent speakers have. Although my stammer is still there, I realise I cannot blame it for all the adversities of life, and having been at least partially "desensitised" at the City Lit, probably am only slightly more tense and anxious than the normal person facing a situation at which he knows he is not adept.

I certainly don't feel helpless anymore. Although I still have occasional bouts of depression, they are becoming less frequent and I probably get only slightly more depressed than the average person in a given circumstance. Remember, before my speech became more fluent, I had all the normal person's hangups and problems plus those associated with my speech. Now my problems and worries are mainly only those of the normal, fluent person.

Whilst acknowledging and accepting that I am still abnormal (don't forget I'm one of the one percent of the population who stammers), I'm only a victim of the problems and feelings I have imposed upon myself - not a victim of my "enemies". So what's there to feel suicidal about? If I do jump out of a skyscraper, it won't be because of stammering (or the Marge Ryans of this world).

I feel now that perhaps my enemies weren't prejudiced after all. Uncomprehending and impatient might be better words. That's my answer for stammerers who feel prejudiced against. I wish I had as simple an answer to that for racial and other prejudices. But I'm working on one.

So I now press on with hope and confidence, not despair and frustration. Just putting down on paper my lifetime feelings of frustration, anger and finally hope and confidence, has been therapeutic and cathartic in itself. It was a year ago when Jan Anderson made me play those silly games. Since then, although I have not conquered the blight that pained my family, friends and myself for fifty-five years, I am mastering it and the world is a better home.

I hope this little book will spread a touch of understanding, patience and comprehension around the fluent-speaking world and a lot of hope among the one per cent who stammer and those who love them.

Now, for me, it's a ferry to Rhodes and then home to London There's a telephone in the village that I can use to call Mary and tell her I'm coming. Alexander Graham Bell, you're a genius.

But no, I'm not doing an audio book.

AFTERWORD

It would be a lie to say that dad never stammered badly again. He did, but without question the serious blocks were far less frequent than they had been. As age and ill health kicked in I think it may have been comfort enough knowing he had the techniques at hand to stammer less, even though he probably found it exhausting to constantly use them. Into his eighties, diminished by various cancers, a stroke and blind, with my mother bedridden from serious ill health, they had far fewer visitors and next to no social life, so dad had little reason to speak to strangers anyway.

After the initial burst of writing this book in the late eighties He often went back to it and tinkered with it. It was never quite right for him and I know he intended to flesh out some of the passages, but which ones I could not say with any certainty. Maybe he would have told us about the many friends he lost to bombs and assassinations in Belfast, and how he had been told more than once that "he would be next", or the time he paid a pilot to fly him out of Viet Nam after being hit with missile shrapnel, turning up covered in blood on our front lawn in the middle of the night. Or the time he covered Muhammad Ali's Thriller In Manilla, and was invited along with mum, Tracey and me to the palace for tea and a private audience with Ferdinand and Imelda Marcos (I asked them where they kept their gold, then fell asleep!).

Was it modesty that stopped dad speaking too often about these exciting adventures very often, or his stammer? It doesn't matter now, and though

I'm now a middle-aged father of two myself, I repeat them here as a wide-eyed impressionable young boy would, when talking proudly of his father.

Since dad finished this book I can see that stuttering and stammering have far less of a stigma to them, and as such this book could be seen as something of a timepiece; a reflection of a society that knew far less about speech impediments and how to deal with them than we do now. Nowadays one line of therapy is for stammerers to be proud of their impediment rather than to 'cure' it. Films like The Kings Speech have placed the issue firmly in the spotlight. Joe Biden, elected President of the USA in November 2020, has had a stutter all his life. Moreover, society in general is now more understanding and inclusive of disabilities of all kinds. As such I hope that modern stammerers recognise the time and place the book comes from, and do not find my father's approach to his stammer offensive. At the same time I do appreciate that there is still that moment when we start talking to someone and realise they have a speech impediment. We, all of us, will respond to that moment in different ways. But hopefully this book has shed some light on what the stammerer themselves may be feeling when speaking with the enemy, and through that understanding, can become an ally.

Adam Norsworthy

MY PAPPY

My Pappy has three loves. The first is his family, the second is journalism and the third is New York City. He gets a lot of satisfaction out of his work and he thinks he got the most out of covering the fighting in Northern Ireland. My Grandma says that Pappy went over to Northern Ireland for the weekend and stayed for two years. Northern Ireland is a part of the UK but Ireland claims it but the British won't let go of it, and the IRA (who are mainly Catholics) are trying to get the British out, or at least, get Northern Ireland under the Irish government and not the government in London. Pappy met a lot of IRA people in the flesh and he said they were charming, and that you wouldn't think they were the kind of people to leave bombs in crowded restaurants and kill lots of people. So Pappy's liking for these people was evened out by the dead bodies he saw. Some of the bombs were put in hotels where journalists were staying. Although the IRA liked journalists, they liked to scare them and to try and make sure they would write nice things. Some journalists were afraid to write anything bad about the IRA but my Pappy wrote what he believed. He found the job satisfying but said it was always nice to come home. He enjoyed getting on the plane, knowing he was leaving the bombs and the killing behind him.

There was one time Pappy got on the plane and he sat back and ordered a gin and tonic and he looked down the aisle as the plane was going taking off and a brief case slid down the aisle. The IRA had warned they were going to bomb planes but the journalists didn't think they were really going to do it, but the suitcase coming down the aisle was scary. So Pappy called out to people around him asking who owned it. Nobody said anything so he called the air stewardess and said "excuse me, there is a brief case here that nobody is claiming and it is scaring the hell out of me". She agreed and went off to tell the captain who came on the loud-speaker and asked everybody if they owned the suitcase in the aisle. Nobody said anything. The captain turned the plane around back to Ireland where there were fire engines, the army and the police with guns waiting at the airport. The passengers were told to leave the plane quickly, and as they were leaving the plane a man said "hello there, has anyone seen my brief case?" My Pappy wondered why the army hadn't shot him there and then! He must have been asleep!

By this time, Pappy had lived in three countries. Britain, Ireland and USA. But Singapore was thousands of miles from his home and it was going to be a new experience for Mary, Tracey and Adam and Pappy! He had come to England when he was thirty years old and single, and he had no plans to marry. He had gone to work for Reuters International News Agency as a journalist and he became friends with some fellow journalists at Reuters who seemed to hang around pubs a lot. One day he walked into a pub in Notting hill Gate and there was a girl talking to a friend of his. They were introduced and a month later they got married. That girl was my Grandma! Now Grandma and Pappy have two children and four grandchildren. A far cry from his 'halcyon days' in Notting hill Gate!

In Singapore, life for Pappy seemed to go on as usual. He would go into the office every day and the only thing different was that the people around him were mostly Chinese. However, for Grandma and the children, life changed. They were able to afford an Ahma, which is a servant, and Grandma found time to play tennis and learn how to play bridge. There were times when Pappy had to leave Singapore and travel around Asia. Pappy said the two most exciting places he went to were Vietnam and Cambodia. They are part of the three Asian countries called Indo China (the other is Laos) and they were all at one time run by France.

Cambodia is like Vietnam and there was a war on there at the time. It was part of the same war that was going on in Vietnam. The food in Vietnam was part French and part Chinese and Pappy said it was the best food he had ever had in his life.

In Cambodia, life was very different. The people were starving and being bombed every day by communist forces. Communism is a form of politics. My Pappy has told me not to get into this! The rockets started early in the day and went on through the night. There were explosions all day long. One day a rocket hit a girl's school and killed six girls about my age. There had been two rocket explosions and Pappy had gone to see what had happened. When the bomb hit the girls' school, Pappy was there because he had gone to the first explosion. At the school there was a brick wall and there were cars parked against the wall which he tried to use for cover. When the second rocket went off he heard it coming. Pappy took a dive and landed on a girl about my age. It was clear she went to this private school and she could speak English. They got up and Pappy apologised and this ten year old girl said "that is alright, you would have been killed and not me if the explosion had reached us" and Pappy thought that for a girl that age to say something as cool as that was a sign of what war could do to people.

His arms and chest and hands were scraped and raw and bleeding. Pappy looked around and there were people lying on the ground bleeding and dying. The ambulances came and they opened the back door of the ambulance and just started throwing people in. Pappy was very dazed but he asked a friend why they were being so rough and in such a hurry. The friend replied that the Khmer Rouge (the enemy) fire rockets into town and then all the fire engines and ambulances and the army arrive and then they fire again and hit all the people who go to help so that is why throw they them in in a hurry and drive away before the next round of rockets comes in.

Once when he was walking in Phnom Penh, the capital of Cambodia, he saw a man in a white suit looking really smart. Then a bomb went off and Pappy saw him being thrown into an ambulance and his smart white suit was completely red with blood.

Pappy got back to the hotel and he was bleeding badly and some of his skin was coming off, so he went to a hospital and he walked in and there were people lying on the floors dying. Pappy decided his injuries were not bad enough to deprive any of those people medical treatment. So to get out of the way he just went back to his hotel and took aspirin and he finally got to sleep that night. He was having bad nightmares so he finally turned on the light and saw he was black with flies all over him because of his injuries! Pappy went crazy! All the foreigners decided it was time to leave Cambodia, only the airport had shut down because of the bombs which were falling on it. So Reuters told Pappy that he could spend anything to get a plane home. However, he could not buy himself a flight as the runway was closed. The army had pushed the enemy back but the airports were still closed. Luckily the American embassy (every country has an office in other countries and these offices are called embassies and if you are in trouble in a foreign country, you go to the embassy of your country) managed to get an aeroplane to take Americans out of Cambodia. The problem was that the airport was still being bombed. The plane was parked just out of range of the bombs. My Pappy had to run through the bombs with everyone else to get to the plane, dodging them as they went! Luckily he got to the plane and it took him home.

When he got back to London he started to fly around the world for Reuters and he went to Belgrade which is what is now known as Serbia. Pappy arrived by train. An old man walked up to him and asked if he wanted a taxi. Pappy replied "yes please" and the man asked pappy which hotel he was staying in. The man hoisted his suitcase on his shoulder and said "follow me". So Pappy followed and he crossed the street and kept on walking and Pappy thought this taxi is a long way away, so they walked and walked and walked and finally he put the suitcase down and the man said "here we are"! He didn't have a taxi at all, he had carried the suitcase the whole way to Pappy's hotel! He then asked for ten dollars. My Pappy said "what? that is a lot of money". The man said that he had had to carry the bag all that way! It turned out a taxi would have cost $2 but the man had charged $10. My Pappy had been had!

Pappy went to Savannah High school which should have been a fun time. Everybody else enjoyed it except Pappy, and that is because of his stammer. He said the teachers were not very nice about it, and that they didn't help him at all. They thought it was his own fault and that he should "pull his socks up". Pappy's stammer has plagued him every moment of his life. Every job he did was achieved despite his stammer. Pappy said his stammer made a good life out of what could have been a wonderful life.

While he was in Savannah he was a copy boy and then a junior reporter on a local newspaper. But Pappy wanted the good life so he went to New York and got a job on a news agency there. He *loved* New York! He worked a lot of shift work and no matter what time he got off work, New York was always moving. Buzz, buzz, things were always happening. You could do anything at any time. You could go to the cinema or to a restaurant at 4am. Pappy loved it! Pappy was working on a newspaper in New Jersey which is right next to New York and he had always wanted to go abroad and there was an advertisement in the paper for a journalist to come to London and work for Reuters, and he decided to try it. There were about two hundred people applying for that job but my Pappy got the job! He decided to stay in London for a year, and then he would travel around a bit on his holidays, and then he would go back to New York.. but he is still here! And that was 1962, 48 years ago!

Pappy retired from Reuters but they called him back to teach young journalists. Pappy enjoyed that a lot because he was surrounded with young graduates who asked intelligent questions and who went a long way towards keeping Pappy's brain working! Pappy then went to work for a charity shop which he enjoyed for four years. And then Pappy had to stop as he had a stroke. He recovered quite well from this. In fact, so well that another charity asked him to go to a country called Laos and help run an English language newspaper there. So Pappy was in Laos for three months. Laos is near Vietnam and Cambodia. He brought me back a green dress and a peasant's hat which I loved. I wore it all the time!

One of the student journalists summed it up in an in-house magazine by describing Pappy as the world's greatest and grumpiest journalist. My Pappy is the most interesting person in the whole wide world and I love him.

Eleanor Lawrie, niece
2010, aged 10

ACKNOWLEDGEMENTS

I'm afraid these acknowledgements come more from me than from dad, as he never got round to officially making them. But I know for certain that the first person he would like to thank is Lesley Saltmarsh, who sat with him for many hours going through passages in this book. Lesley once confessed to me that she did it as much to spend quality time with dad, as to help him with the writing, and I know dad treasured their time together. She was the first person I sent my edited version to, and I would also like to say a huge thank you to her, as well as her husband Bill, both of whom remain close and valued friends to this day.

Dad would have also no doubt liked to thank Mary Thomas, and acknowledge the encouragement of her late husband Alan as well.

There are too many therapists from the City Lit for me to know by name, but as an institution I'm sure by you know by now the depth of gratitude dad had for the place. In the book he mentions Tom Reid, Carolyn Cheasman and Jan Anderson in particular, but I'm sure there were many others who helped dad with his speech.

Dad would also certainly want to acknowledge Tim Newark, from whose book "Not Good At Talking' he has quoted.

I would personally like to thank Elaine Kelman from the Michael Palin Institute and Oliver Dimsdale for their expert advice, guidance and encouragement.

Finally, a thank you from both my sister Tracey and I to our mother, Mary, whom we lost four months to the day after dad, to the coronavirus. There are few people more loving and full of life than mum was. I never once heard her mention dad's speech in frustration or anger, or even pity. She loved dad completely and they were a perfect team. They were married for almost fifty-six years.

I have absolutely no doubt he would have dedicated this book to her, and Tracey and I want to thank them both, for absolutely everything.